Frederick Law Olmsted

Twayne's World Leaders Series

Arthur Brown, Editor
University of Miami, Coral Gables, Florida

TWLS 83

FREDERICK LAW OLMSTED
Photograph of Olmsted in his later years by James Notman, as engraved by T. Johnson, originally published in the *Century Magazine*.

(Courtesy of the Stokes Autograph Collection, Yale University Library)

Frederick Law Olmsted

By John Emerson Todd

Baruch College, City University of New York

Twayne Publishers • Boston

Frederick Law Olmsted

John Emerson Todd

Copyright © 1982 by G. K. Hall & Co.
Published by Twayne Publishers
A Division of G. K. Hall & Company
70 Lincoln Street
Boston, Massachusetts 02111

Book production by Marne Sultz
Book design by Barbara Anderson

Printed on permanent/durable
acid-free paper and bound in
The United States of America

Library of Congress Cataloging in Publication Data

Todd, John Emerson.
Frederick Law Olmsted.

(Twayne's world leaders series; TWLS 83)
Bibliography: p. 199
Includes index.
1. Olmsted, Frederick Law, 1822–1903.
2. Landscape architects—United States—Biography.
I. Title. II. Series.
SB470.05T63   712'.092'4[B]   81-13189
ISBN 0-8057-7729-6   AACR2

2164076

Contents

About the Author

John Emerson Todd received a B.A. from Oberlin College, an M.A. from Columbia University, and a Ph.D. in English from the University of Wisconsin. Having taught at the University of Michigan and the University of Arizona, he is currently associate professor of English at Baruch College, the City University of New York.

He is the author of *Emily Dickinson's Use of the Persona* (The Hague: Mouton, 1973), articles on American literature and New York City history, and numerous book reviews. He served for five years as a member of the Modern Language Association Committee on Bibliography in American Literature.

Preface

It has taken Frederick Law Olmsted a long time to gain his rightful place as one of the distinguished and influential leaders in America during the nineteenth century. During his lifetime he came to be acknowledged as the father of landscape architecture in this country. He achieved considerable fame for his contributions to parks and park systems in over a dozen major cities, including both Central and Prospect parks in New York City. He also contributed significantly to the preservation of scenic landmarks like Yosemite National Park and Niagara Falls, to the development of the first scientifically managed forest in the United States, to the landscaping of the great Columbian Exposition of 1893, to the planning of model suburban communities, to the design of numerous college campuses throughout the country, and to the laying out of estates such as George W. Vanderbilt's vast Biltmore acreage near Asheville, North Carolina.

Yet within several decades after his death in 1903, Olmsted was half forgotten, no doubt partly because of the very nature of his accomplishments. At the very height of his contemporary success in the last decade of his life, *Garden and Forest*, a magazine that he had helped to found, declared prophetically that, although he was the "foremost artist which the New World has yet produced," his memory "may be dimmed in the passage of years, for it is the fate of architects to be lost in their work."[1] Architecture, and especially landscape architecture, often tend to be taken for granted. In addition, however, fate has been even more unkind to most of Olmsted's works—especially his urban parks—which have suffered severe neglect and mutilation in the twentieth century.

In the 1930s, a brief chapter in Lewis Mumford's *The Brown Decades* helped to rescue Olmsted's career from the oblivion into which it had largely fallen. In recent years, especially with the one hundred and fiftieth anniversary of his birth in 1972, interest in him has quickened enormously, and for a variety of reasons. An extensive collection of letters and documents, many of them written by Olmsted, his family, and his friends, was opened to the public for the first time at the Library of Congress in Washington, D.C., after having been held restrictively for nearly fifty years. But a more important reason for this renewed interest in his work is undoubtedly the current preoccupation with ecology and the conservation of America's natural resources. As interest in large-scale urban and ecological planning has increased, it is only natural that the founder of the profession of landscape architecture should be heralded anew and justly appreciated as the most comprehensive environmental planner and designer that America has produced.

The 1970s saw the appearance of two biographies of Olmsted, both based upon the newly available materials in the collection that Olmsted's son, Frederick Law Olmsted, Jr., foresightedly put together for the Library of Congress. Laura Wood Roper had access to the collection before it was opened to other scholars, and her *FLO: A Biography of Frederick Law Olmsted* (1973) is a monumental, painstaking account of the events of a remarkable life. Elizabeth Stevenson's *Park Maker: A Life of Frederick Law Olmsted* (1977) began with her interest in Olmsted as a nineteenth-century conservationist concerned with the transformation of the environment. She provides a vividly personalized narrative of a man pulled by the conflicting claims of nature and art. Then, too, Charles Capen McLaughlin and his associates are at work on a multivolume edition of the Olmsted papers that will make easily available many previously little-known details of Olmsted's life. The first volume of this edition, tracing Olmsted's formative years from 1822 to 1852, appeared in 1977.

My book has a somewhat different objective from these previous biographies and from McLaughlin's edition of the Olmsted papers. After a general introductory chapter dealing with Olmsted's life and several careers, my work turns to what I have tried to make a systematic consideration of his specific achievements. Although diverse and seemingly unrelated on first inspection, these achievements, both major and minor, demonstrate something of an underlying unity.

Even though Olmsted never deliberately prepared for what was to be a great career as a landscape architect, his restless drifting in his youth and early manhood from one endeavor to another proves in retrospect to have been the ideal training for his later work. It is interesting to watch the cumulative development of his career over the early decades of his life. Although he was what would today be called a late bloomer, very little of what he experienced was lost on him. Thus his earliest career as a scientific farmer laid a solid foundation, for example, for his later interest in scientific social planning.

Olmsted had, in fact, a remarkable talent for putting all his previous experiences to work in any new enterprise. Part of the fascination I discovered in attempting to sort out his various careers was in examining the interrelated threads running throughout his life, including those of his classic journalism in chronicling the slave-powered plantations of the antebellum South and of his interlude as head of the Sanitary Commission for the Union Army during the Civil War. Threads like these continually strengthened the whole fabric of his life while adding color and variety to the individual undertakings.

John Emerson Todd

Baruch College, City University of New York

Acknowledgments

I am grateful to a number of people and institutions for their help in the preparation of this manuscript. In particular, I want to thank the following: my editor, Arthur W. Brown, dean of the College of Arts and Sciences, University of Miami, Coral Gables, for his skillful guidance in helping plan the project initially and for his constant support and encouragement; John C. Broderick and his staff, Manuscript Division, Library of Congress, for counsel and the use of the Frederick Law Olmsted papers and supplementary papers; and the Photoduplication Service, Library of Congress, for the fifty-one reels of microfilm containing these papers, available through interlibrary loan; the Manuscripts and Archives Division, New York Public Library, Astor, Lenox and Tilden Foundations, for the use of materials from the Calvert Vaux papers; Henry Hope Reed, former curator of Central Park, for the benefit of his knowledge of the New York parks and of the personalities of Olmsted and Vaux, and for suggestions of areas for research; members of the Friends of Central Park for their enthusiasm about Olmsted and for walking tours and other events held periodically in the park; Professor Elaine M. Kauvar, colleague and friend, for inspiration and guidance; my sister, Virginia Todd Schatzki, for assistance in obtaining information about a report Olmsted wrote regarding the laying out of plots for summer residences on Cushing Island off the coast of Portland, Maine; my cousin, Stanton W. Todd, Jr., for his enthusiastic support of the project; Robert Lindquist, a family friend of long standing, for helpful information about Olmsted's design for Riverside, Illinois, the suburb where I spent eight pleasant years of my boyhood; Daniel J. Knutson, for constant inspiration and patient understanding.

Chronology

1822 Frederick Law Olmsted born on 26 April in Hartford, Connecticut.

1826 Begins schooling at the local dame schools in Hartford.

1836 Suffers severe sumac poisoning, causing temporary partial blindness.

1837 Studies civil engineering with Frederick A. Barton in Andover, Massachusetts.

1840 Works in New York City for dry-goods importing firm of Benkard and Hutton.

1843 Ships as apprentice seaman on bark *Ronaldson*, bound for Canton.

1845 Attends lectures of Professor Benjamin Silliman at Yale College.

1846 Serves as apprentice on George Geddes's model farm near Syracuse, New York.

1847 Farms at Sachem's Head, Guilford, Connecticut.

1848 Moves to better farm on south shore of Staten Island, New York.

1850 Leaves for walking trip through England with brother John and Charles Loring Brace.

1852 *Walks and Talks of an American Farmer in England.* Starts on southern tour as journalist for *New-York Daily Times.*

1855 Becomes partner in firm of Dix and Edwards, publishers of *Putnam's Monthly Magazine.*

1856 *A Journey in the Seaboard Slave States.*

1857 Appointed superintendent of Central Park in New York City. *A Journey through Texas; or, a Saddle-Trip on the Southwestern Frontier.*

1858 Wins first prize, with Calvert Vaux, in competition for Central Park design. Named architect in chief of Central Park.

1859 Marries Mary Cleveland Perkins Olmsted, his brother's widow.

1860 *A Journey in the Back Country.*

1861 Appointed executive secretary of the United States Sanitary Commission. *The Cotton Kingdom.*

1863 Accepts superintendency of the Mariposa Estate, a large gold mining property in California.

1864 Designated a commissioner to help establish Yosemite Park.

1865 Reappointed, with Vaux, landscape architects for Central Park. Appointed, with Vaux, to design Prospect Park in Brooklyn.

1868 Lays out, with Vaux, model suburban village at Riverside, Illinois. Enters into negotiations about major park project in Buffalo.

1869 Becomes concerned about preservation of Niagara Falls.

1870 Initiates organization for comprehensive improvement of Staten Island.

1872 Dissolves partnership with Calvert Vaux.

1874 Engaged to plan Mount Royal Park for Montreal. Appointed landscape architect for the U.S. Capitol in Washington, D.C.

1875 Begins work on "emerald necklace" park system for Boston.

1876 Serves on advisory board for new state capitol building at Albany.

1878 Dismissed from position with New York City Department of Public Parks for political reasons.

1881 Begins preparing plan for Belle Isle Park in Detroit.

1883 Makes permanent move from New York City to Brookline, Massachusetts, which becomes his professional headquarters and home.

1885 Prepares final design for Franklin Park in Boston.

1886 Asked to plan grounds of Stanford University at Palo Alto, California.

1888 Begins design of George W. Vanderbilt's mountain estate, Biltmore, near Asheville, North Carolina. Helps found periodical *Garden and Forest.*

1890   Begins laying out grounds for World's Columbian Exposition of 1893 in Chicago.
1893   Receives honorary degree of Doctor of Laws from both Harvard and Yale.
1895   Retires from professional practice.
1903   Dies on 28 August at McLean Hospital in Waverley, Massachusetts.

Chapter One

The Life and Careers

Background and Early Life

Frederick Law Olmsted, the first child of John Olmsted and Charlotte Law Hull, was born on 26 April 1822, in the small but already thriving New England city of Hartford, Connecticut. Some of his ancestors had helped to found Hartford during the seventeenth century. James Olmsted, the first member of the family to emigrate to the New World from Essex, England, became an original proprietor in Hartford. Sharing in the land distribution of 1639, he received seventy acres on the road that later became Front Street. The Olmsted family prospered from the beginning of their settlement in Hartford. Nicholas, James's son, served as an officer in the wars against the Indians and as deputy to the General Court, managing to acquire considerable land on both sides of the Connecticut River. Succeeding generations included farmers, soldiers, patriots, and seafaring men in the China trade.

John, Olmsted's father, was a successful, well-established owner of a large dry-goods store in Hartford. With only a common school education, he achieved a solid reputation there, becoming a member of the fire department and an aide de camp to the general of militia. Though never really a prominent figure because of a strong modesty in his nature, he was an altruistic, civic-minded citizen, becoming a director of the Hartford Retreat for the Insane and a trustee of the Wadsworth Atheneum. Olmsted's mother, Charlotte, came from Cheshire, Connecticut. Because she died when he was only three years old, he remembered almost nothing about her. John Olmsted, left with two young sons, Frederick Law and John Hull, soon mar-

ried Mary Ann Bull, an efficient and devoutly religious woman of
Hartford who had been a friend of Charlotte.

Partly from his father and stepmother, Olmsted early developed a
love of travel and a responsiveness to the gentle rural landscape
around Hartford. Travel was his father's principal recreation, and
throughout his life John Olmsted liked to take leisurely trips around
the region of the Connecticut Valley, though, characteristically, he
rarely expressed his reactions to them. It is little wonder, then, that,
by the time Olmsted was twelve, he had seen most of New England
as well as West Point, Lake George, Niagara Falls, and Quebec.

His formal schooling was desultory and sporadic, beginning when
he was four at local dame schools. John Olmsted, ambitious for his
sons and intending to prepare them for Yale, nevertheless did not
trust his own instincts in raising them. As a result, Olmsted was
boarded out to a series of clergymen, often having to submit to
rigorous physical discipline and severe discomfort away from home.
A severe case of sumac poisoning, which seriously affected his eyes,
kept him from serious study for a time and ultimately from matricu-
lation at Yale. In all, he was moved twelve times before his ele-
mentary and high school education was considered complete in 1840.

Even before the sumac poisoning, however, Olmsted loved to
wander around the Hartford countryside to visit a variety of family
relatives and friends. It was not considered unusual when he and
his brother, aged nine and six respectively, walked sixteen miles
over country new to them to see their uncle and aunt. They were
on the road for two days and spent a night in a rural inn. Olmsted
enjoyed being outdoors more than at his lessons, yet he was exposed
to a good deal of literature not only through his schooling but in
poking around in the libraries of neighbors and relatives like his
scholarly uncle Jonathan Law, friend of John Greenleaf Whittier,
who read to him from the Latin poets. Somewhere he found prints
of English park scenery, and his interest in them led him to discover
such eighteenth-century English writers on the picturesque as Uvedale Price and William Gilpin, who had instructed the British
gentry on how to appreciate scenery on their travels.

Because Olmsted was advised to spend as much time outdoors as possible until his eyes improved, he was sent off to study civil engineering with Frederick Augustus Barton in Andover, Massachusetts. There he learned the fundamentals of surveying and also spent time fishing, hunting, and collecting rocks and plants. After this experience, his father tried to make a merchant of him by sending him to clerk in New York City at Benkard and Hutton, French dry-goods importers. Although Olmsted spent eighteen months there, he developed no liking for business. He did, however, become familiar with the wharves and ships of the city while checking consignments of dry goods. This experience may have been partly responsible for his decision, when he was twenty, to sail to China as a seaman. His brother John had entered Yale in 1842, and he was left at loose ends, undecided on a career.

Richard Henry Dana, Jr., had created a stir several years earlier with *Two Years Before the Mast*, his account of the tremendous hardships of a seaman's life on a voyage to California. Herman Melville, though unknown to Olmsted, had already shipped out on a whaler, bound for the Pacific and a three-year adventure that was to shape his life and writing. In the 1840s it was not uncommon for young men from good homes to go to sea for a while, especially when, as in Olmsted's case, the seafaring tradition ran strong in the family. Undaunted by his reading of Dana's book, Olmsted returned to New York to find a berth on a ship. Since he had never been to sea before, he could qualify only as an apprentice seaman on the *Ronaldson*, an American ship in the China trade. He was miserably seasick on the rough voyage across the Atlantic toward the Cape of Good Hope, and the captain proved a tyrant with little concern for his crew's welfare at sea. A conscientious sailor, Olmsted was able to escape punishment throughout his voyage, but the abuse of many other members of the crew impressed him to the point that he later publicly denounced the absolutism granted ships' captains.

The *Ronaldson* finally reached Hong Kong but remained there only briefly because no market existed for its goods and the city was fever ridden. Olmsted was frequently frustrated in his attempts to find the adventure for which he had come and made only three brief visits ashore at the next port, Canton. Though, strangely, he

never mentioned in his letters home the appearance of Canton or
the Chinese countryside, he did comment on the general courtesy
of the Chinese toward foreigners, despite the provocations of the
recent Opium War between the Chinese and British. The return
trip proved worse, if anything, than the voyage across. The ship,
laden with a cargo of tea, cassia, and raw silk, was shorthanded, and
the crew, badly overworked, almost mutinied. John Olmsted literally
did not recognize his emaciated son when the ship landed in New
York after almost a year.

After spending a summer recuperating, Olmsted decided to turn
his hand to farming. Recognizing the need for scientific knowledge
if he was to pursue this occupation, he audited some lectures at Yale
for a time. He probably learned something about chemistry and
scientific agriculture from Benjamin Silliman. In New Haven he
also met a girl who had a deep influence on him, though no close
friendship seems to have developed. At a time when he was feeling
badly educated, Elizabeth Wooster Baldwin, attractive daughter of
Roger Sherman Baldwin, recent governor of Connecticut, persuaded
him that his lack of a formal education need not prevent him from
becoming an intelligent and cultured man. She seems to have introduced him to the writings of Emerson, Lowell, and Ruskin.

He next found a position as apprentice on a model farm belong-
ing to George Geddes near Syracuse, New York. Geddes, whose
father had been engineer of the Erie Canal, had created a prize-
winning farm well recognized for its productiveness and quality.
Olmsted soon gained confidence in his ability to farm but was lonely
away from his home and friends. He became interested in a little
farm at Sachem's Head on the coast of Connecticut, and his father
bought it for him. He spent the year 1847 improving the run-down
condition of the farm but soon came to realize that it was too small,
rocky, and infertile to be a commercial success. At the beginning of
1848, therefore, his father bought him, on the south shore of Staten
Island, a much better farm that he spent the next two years developing.

The view from the farmhouse took in the whole lower bay of
New York, including the lighthouse on Sandy Hook and the west

end of Long Island. Showing increasing talent for administration and landscape design, Olmsted transformed the run-down grounds into a gentleman's country seat. His improvements included moving the barns out of sight behind a knoll and laying out a new three-quarter mile drive so that it approached the house in a graceful curve. A strict system began to appear in his method of operation: he required his hired men to do their chores on an hourly schedule and his foreman to report on the day's progress regularly before supper in the evening. Frequently working alongside his men, he enthusiastically planted a variety of trees and set out a pear orchard. During this period he became a man of some prominence on Staten Island, serving as a trustee on the school board and working with other leading farmers toward a county agricultural society. Having drawn up the constitution, he was elected corresponding secretary.

In the spring of 1850, when his brother John planned a walking trip through England with Charles Loring Brace, who had been his roommate at Yale, Olmsted longed to go with them. For many years, he indicated in a letter to his father, he had been filled with a passion to travel abroad, and he argued that the experience of observing English agricultural methods would be worth money to him afterward. His father agreed to let him go along, and the three young men sailed for Liverpool at the end of April. Once in England, Olmsted admired the agricultural practices in the regions through which they passed, but his greatest interest was in the delightful scenery of the English countryside. It was the commonplace rural landscape with no really grandiose or distinguished features that fascinated him most. Another interest he developed was in the condition of the poorer classes of citizens, especially farm laborers. He showed no particular desire to meet members of the aristocracy in England. The luxurious trappings of the great private estates appealed to his aesthetic taste but tended to offend his moral sensibilities. These interests converged when he inspected the new rural park at Birkenhead, across the Mersey River from Liverpool. This was the first public park he had ever seen, and it was a revelation to him. Here Joseph Paxton, future designer of the revolutionary Crystal Palace of 1851, had taken 125 acres of farmland and turned them into a public park for Birkenhead citizens of every class, who flocked there to enjoy the restful surroundings. During the rest of his trip, Olmsted was less impressed with the private parks he saw than with these public recreation grounds.

The Olmsted brothers arrived home at the end of six months abroad, having spent one month on the continent in France, Holland, Belgium, and Germany. Brace stayed on in Europe, paying the expenses of his trip by sending back travel letters to New York and Philadelphia newspapers. Olmsted likewise began collecting the detailed letters he had written home from England and decided to put together a book from them. He could use the income but, more than that, felt the publication of such a book would give him an influence on his contemporaries that he wanted. *Walks and Talks of an American Farmer in England* was published in two volumes in 1852. Although well received, it did not have the initial impact he hoped for. Yet it served to gain him admittance to the best intellectual circles of New York.

In the meantime, both Olmsted and his brother had become engaged to be married to unrelated girls by the name of Perkins, he to Emily Perkins and John to Mary Cleveland Bryant Perkins. John and Mary were married on schedule even though John was found to be suffering from tuberculosis. Olmsted's engagement, however, was abruptly broken off by a letter from Emily Perkins's mother reporting that her daughter had had a change of heart. Emily soon after met her future husband, Edward Everett Hale, who was becoming a leading Unitarian minister. Olmsted was stunned by the experience, though it is a question whether he was actually heartbroken. He kept busy by writing a long article entitled "A Voice from the Sea" that was published in the *American Whig Review*. Still angry at the barbarous treatment of sailors he had experienced on his voyage to China, he proposed the establishment of schools to educate seafaring men in the arts of seamanship and in habits of order and discipline. Implicit, too, in his proposal was his already firm belief in the value of recreation, including the kind that could be provided by free public parks and gardens, in improving the sailor's lot while he was ashore.

Olmsted's writings brought him to the attention of Henry J. Raymond, editor of the year-old *New-York Daily Times*, who was looking for a correspondent to tour the South and send back letters on southern agriculture and the economic aspects of slavery. Harriet Beecher Stowe's sentimental novel *Uncle Tom's Cabin* had recently been published, and Raymond wanted to counter her presentation with objective firsthand observation of conditions in the South. Interested in reporting that would be independent of the editorial position of the *Times*, he did not even inquire into Olmsted's views on slavery. Olmsted accepted the assignment and started south in December 1852 on a four months' journey through the slave states. Traveling from Washington to New Orleans and then home again by stagecoach, rail, and steamboat, with frequent excursions on horseback as well, he tirelessly gave a wealth of detail wherever he went about manners and dress of the natives, construction and furnishings of buildings, management of plantations, and methods of agriculture. He also challenged the myth that southern chivalry and gentility were a creative force justifying the institution of slavery. He found the South, instead, a stagnant society employing slave labor that was an economic handicap to agricultural and industrial progress.

The *Times* launched Olmsted's letters in 1853 under the pseudonym Yeoman, and the series ran for a full year. On his return, he had not only to manage his farm on Staten Island but to work up his material for the paper. He was increasingly attracted to the life of a writer, and before long he and his brother John had drawn up an ambitious itinerary designed to take them, by way of Texas, across the continent to California. Olmsted would send back to the *Times* more letters on his experiences. The brothers started out in November 1853 by way of Cincinnati and New Orleans, to San Antonio, where they intended to await the formation of a larger group for the dangerous trip to California. They were forced, finally, to abandon their plans to go farther west when the route was blocked by a tribe of Lipan Indians on the warpath. Instead, they made a trip through the western Texas border country into Mexico with a Texas Ranger for a guide. Then they started home, John on a steamer from New

Orleans to New York and the indefatigable Frederick alone on horseback through the infrequently visited southern hill country.

After arriving home in August 1854 Olmsted continued to contribute articles and letters to the *Times*. He was becoming increasingly engaged in the political and social issues of the decade before the Civil War. He did not become a wholehearted abolitionist but was a gradualist, attempting to persuade slave owners that it would be to their interest to change to a free labor system. He also actively supported the Free Soil parties in Texas and Kansas. At the same time, he was looking around for another literary connection that would give him additional influence and found it in the spring of 1855, when he was asked to become a partner in Dix and Edwards, a firm that published *Putnam's Monthly Magazine*. Olmsted's capital was needed in the firm, and he had to persuade his father to lend him $5,000. He did not make the major editorial decisions but served as a kind of front man, dealing with writers, correspondence, and public relations. The literary quality of the newly established *Putnam's Monthly* was high, and he had the opportunity to meet such contributors as Emerson, Longfellow, Lowell, and Thackeray.

Olmsted had expanded his articles on the seaboard South into a book and needed a thousand dollars more from his father before it appeared in January 1856 as *A Journey in the Seaboard Slave States*. The book was not a commercial success but was widely acclaimed, except in the South, because of its spotlight on slavery from an economic rather than a primarily humanitarian perspective. On business for Dix and Edwards, he sailed to England to persuade prominent publishers in London to make consignments to the firm, his book just beginning to attract attention there. But after empowering him to commit the firm to foreign royalty payments in return for the right to publish overseas authors in the United States, Dix and Edwards failed to honor the commitments Olmsted had made, because of rapidly deteriorating finances. By the time he returned to New York, it was close to ruin.

His brother John was slowly dying of tuberculosis but was able, in his last year of life, to expand Olmsted's Texas notes and letters into a book, *A Journey through Texas; or, a Saddle-Trip on the*

Southwestern Frontier. Dix and Edwards barely managed to publish the work—ironically, another critical success—in January 1857, before going bankrupt in the financial crisis that year. Olmsted was so deeply disappointed by the failure of his publishing venture that he avoided talking about it the rest of his life. He no longer had enough interest in his Staten Island farm to make it pay and had to find other means of supporting himself and paying off the debts to his father.

Great Opportunity: Central Park

The opportunity of a lifetime came to him in August 1857 while he was vacationing at a seaside inn at Morris Cove, Connecticut. He happened to encounter Charles W. Elliott, one of the commissioners of the newly designated landscaping project in the middle of Manhattan that was to become Central Park. Elliott mentioned that a superintendent was soon to be appointed to manage both the labor force building the park and the park police, and he urged Olmsted to apply for the job. Setting out for New York that same evening, Olmsted arrived the next day and began collecting signatures for a petition to the Central Park Commission. Because of his reputation as a writer and his acquaintance with prominent people, he had no difficulty obtaining a large number of sponsors. Some objection developed among the commissioners that, because he was a literary man, he might lack the practical skill needed to direct labor and police in the park, but he was finally selected.

Little in Olmsted's previous record would have indicated his superb talent as the administrator of what was then the largest public work in New York. He had moved restlessly from one interest to another, always indulged and supported by his patient father, for more than a dozen years. He was now thirty-five years old, feeling bitterly humiliated by his aborted publishing career and at that age starting a new job that paid a salary of only $1,500 a year. Almost desperately he threw himself into his work on the treeless and rocky tract. And yet, without having deliberately prepared for his job, he had acquired just those abilities and qualities of mind that enabled him to convert the chaotic work force in Central Park into a smoothly functioning machine.

As Olmsted superintended the vast operation of clearing the land, he became closely associated with the man who was to exert the strongest influence on his professional life. An Englishman by birth, Calvert Vaux had come to the United States as architectural assistant to Andrew Jackson Downing, the nationally prominent landscape gardener of Newburgh, New York. After Downing's tragic death by drowning in 1852, Vaux had inherited his practice. Downing had been influential, along with William Cullen Bryant, poet and editor of the *New York Evening Post*, in calling attention to the need for a great public park in New York City, and Vaux continued Downing's interest. When the commissioners announced a public competition for a park design, Vaux invited Olmsted to collaborate on a plan, and the two men worked together at night for several months on "Greensward" before submitting it on the last day of the competition, 1 April 1858. The last of thirty-three entries, "Greensward" won first prize.

The intention of Olmsted and Vaux was to create contrasting passages of scenery within Central Park, all tending to suggest a great range of English pastoral landscape. Massed foliage was to be used to frame vistas of meadow or greensward. Anticipating the enormous growth of the city, the designers were alone among the contestants in dealing adequately with the problem of accommodating future crosstown traffic and yet keeping it clear of pleasure traffic. The rules of the competition had specified that all plans should provide for at least four direct east-west roads across the park. Olmsted and Vaux brilliantly sank the four required transverse roads beneath the general level of the park, the screening to be done by careful planting. Then, having kept crosstown traffic entirely separate from pleasure traffic, they ingeniously applied the same principle of separation to pleasure traffic itself: the carriage roads would pass over bridle paths and footpaths on bridges, and footpaths and bridle paths would not cross each other at all. Finally, the transverse roads would accommodate crosstown traffic even at night, when Olmsted and Vaux felt the park should be closed.

The two men were equally responsible for the winning design for Central Park. In recognition of Olmsted's previous work as superintendent and his contribution to the "Greensward" plan, however, the commissioners named him architect in chief and raised his salary to $2,500 a year. He was charged with the responsibilities of employing and directing labor and of policing the park. Although problems immediately arose that threatened to prevent him from maintaining the integrity of the plan, especially the constant pressure to grant political favors, his strong insistence on organization and discipline caused the work to progress with amazing speed. Central Park was soon arousing widespread interest not only among New Yorkers but among visitors who came from all over the country to admire and study it. Olmsted could be justly proud of what he was bringing into being: "the first real park made in this country—a democratic development of the highest significance," as he phrased it in a letter to a friend.[1]

He could soon be proud also of something else. His brother John, who had recently died abroad, had left a widow and three small children, who returned to the United States. In a farewell note John had asked of him, "Don't let Mary suffer while you are alive."[2] Olmsted more than fulfilled his obligation when, in June 1859, he and Mary Cleveland Perkins Olmsted were quietly married by Mayor Daniel F. Tiemann in the Bogardus House on Central Park.

His new duties as head of a family of five added heavily to the pressures of professional commitments in the park, where he sometimes directed as many as 3,600 men. His work was made considerably more difficult by Andrew Haswell Green, the commissioner whom the Central Park Board appointed to be their comptroller. With absolute power over all park expenditures, the self-righteous Green was becoming a tyrant, usurping what Olmsted felt was the designers' authority to carry out their plan for Central Park. By the fall of 1859, Olmsted was exhausted. The Park Board granted him a leave of absence, which he used to go abroad by himself to study park design and management in England and on the Continent.

After Olmsted's return, he and Vaux expanded their collaboration beyond the bounds of Central Park. They were engaged to design grounds for the Hartford Retreat for the Insane and to landscape estates in New Rochelle and Roslyn, Long Island. They were also appointed landscape architects and designers to lay out 1,800 acres of rugged terrain in upper Manhattan north of 155th Street. In addition to all the other work, Olmsted found time to complete a third book on his southern travels, *A Journey in the Back Country*, which was published in 1860. The English edition sold so well that the London publishers, Sampson Low, Son and Company, wanted to bring out all three of Olmsted's books in condensed form. On the eve of the Civil War, public demand for accounts of the slave states justified the publication of this additional volume, to be called *The Cotton Kingdom*. Because of his duties on Central Park and elsewhere, Olmsted arranged with Daniel Reeves Goodloe, editor of the abolitionist *National Era* and an authority on the economics of slavery, to help do the condensing for him.

Civil War Years

After the Confederate attack on Fort Sumter touched off the Civil War on 12 April 1861, Olmsted was determined to play a part. He had recently injured his leg badly in a carriage accident that left him lame for years, but he considered it a patriotic duty to support the Union cause. Forming a home guard of the park police, he drilled them on Sundays and encouraged park employees to enlist. He found his real mission, however, as executive secretary of the newly created Sanitary Commission, precursor of the American Red Cross. It was modeled on the British Sanitary Commission, which had performed valuable services during the Crimean War. Taking a leave of absence from Central Park, he went to Washington, D.C., to set up his new office and begin what he later considered his greatest single public service. He recognized the need to apply the most advanced practices of the public health movement of the day to protect the health of the Union forces. Yet the initial report he drew up after his inspection of the camps that had sprung up in the wastelands around Washington was discouraging. Health conditions of the volunteer army were deplorable; the Sanitary Commission, however, had no actual administrative power to institute changes. It could only advise, and its recommendations were frequently not followed.

After the disastrous rout at Bull Run, Olmsted was appalled to discover that the Union army was not only defeated but demoralized. He insisted on the need for greater discipline among the volunteers. Organizing storage depots in large cities where hospital supplies could be collected for shipment to Washington, he joined in hospital inspections as well as tending to his regular duties. The Sanitary Commission accomplished what he considered a major objective when it was instrumental in urging through both houses of Congress a bill reforming the Army Medical Bureau, which had previously been inefficient and obstructive of the Commission's efforts. Olmsted's chief contribution to the passage of the bill was a voluminous report describing the results of nearly four hundred inspections of every branch of the army, along with full recommendations for reform. Dr. William A. Hammond, who became the new surgeon general, carried out many of his suggestions.

During the Peninsula campaign of 1862, Olmsted took charge of equipping and staffing hospital transport ships, which frequently had to be converted from previous use as river steamers. Besides demonstrating superlative administrative skill, he earned the devotion and even affection of his well-chosen subordinates by his fatherly protection of their health and well-being. Women as well as men who served under him as volunteers came to venerate him despite the strict standards on which he insisted. He drove himself relentlessly, often at the sacrifice of his own health. His efforts on the hospital ships helped publicize the work of the Sanitary Commission in the North as nothing before had done. As the ships became familiar sights in northern seaports, funds were more easily raised. Olmsted was also consulted at this turbulent time in the founding of New York's Union League Club. He set forth at length his ideas on what the club should be, stressing that loyalty to freedom and union was not enough to require of its members. Equally important, he thought, was loyalty to the democratic idea and to the "true American aristocracy" of worth and accomplishment.[3]

In 1863 Olmsted was instructed to inspect the Sanitary Commission's operations among Grant's army at the siege of Vicksburg on the Mississippi. The campaign was stalemated when he reached Grant's headquarters above Vicksburg. Invited on board Grant's boat, Olmsted found the general one of the most engaging men he had ever met, partly because of Grant's benevolent attitude toward the Sanitary Commission. In the face of claims by rival relief agencies, the general made two major concessions to the Commission. He ordered that the steamer *Dunleith* be turned over to it for its exclusive use in transporting medical supplies, and he directed that, of all the voluntary relief agencies, only the Commission be given free transportation.

As the war continued, however, Olmsted became disheartened about the role of the Sanitary Commission in it. He felt the Commission was spending too much time on business that did not properly belong to it. In addition, as executive secretary, he disliked having to share responsibility for fiscal control of the Commission's business with members of its executive committee. He felt the same impatience toward his superiors that he had felt as park superintendent. Differences of opinion arose also about how much time Olmsted was expected to spend in the field as opposed to working on organizational plans. In the meantime, Vaux had resigned from the Central Park job because of seemingly irreconcilable differences with Green. Searching about for some new endeavor, Olmsted considered establishing an independent weekly newspaper with Edwin Lawrence Godkin, a rising young journalist. He thought such a paper would be more authoritative than a daily could be and freer of partisan politics.

Robert E. Lee's invasion of the North interrupted his plan, and he was soon back in action. Purchasing and moving supplies to the front in anticipation of the decisive battle of Gettysburg, Olmsted again briefly took over direction of Sanitary Commission operations, working tirelessly through the battle itself. With the tremendous military success at Gettysburg, he thought the time was ripe to launch his new publication when, during a visit to New England, he received a letter that abruptly changed his prospects.

Charles A. Dana, a newspaperman he had known since his days on *Putnam's Monthly*, wrote that the new owners of the Mariposa Estate, a large gold mining property in the foothills of the Sierra Nevada Mountains in California, wanted him for resident manager. Olmsted went immediately to New York to see the estate's owners, who knew his reputation as a brilliant administrator for Central Park and for the Sanitary Commission. The salary of $10,000 a year in gold, plus five hundred shares of stock in the company, appealed to him because he would at last be able to pay off his publishing debts and support his family well. Still, he hesitated about transplanting his family to a miners' village on the wild frontier. But for Olmsted there was usually a higher justification. He reasoned idealistically that, at Mariposa, he would be able to exert an influence "favorable to religion, good order, and civilization."[4] He decided to accept the offer.

California seemed a far distant land. Olmsted sailed alone from New York to the Isthmus of Panama in September 1863, his family to follow the next spring. Traveling by train across the luxuriant isthmus and then sailing along the coast north to San Francisco, he at length arrived at the shabby little village where he was to spend the next two years. His initial reaction to the monotonous brown countryside, suffering from the worst drought in ten years, was bewilderment. The grandeur of the mountains combined with the stunted vegetation was confusing at first to a man accustomed to gentle rural scenery, but he gradually became adapted to the strange beauty of the parched landscape. Beginning to familiarize himself with the extent and business of the Mariposa Estate, including the seven gold mines on the property, he came to understand that the enterprise had been disastrously mismanaged and that the revenue from the mines was declining rapidly. He felt at this time, however, that with better management the property could be made to pay again.

Most essential, in his estimation, was the development of an adequate water supply. He proposed to extend a fork of the Merced River through the estate by means of a canal that would not only prolong mining operations into the dry season but permit agriculture and sheep raising. After reorganizing business operations, Olmsted set out on an exploratory trip into the Sierras for the first time, and his great experience was seeing the Mariposa Big Tree Grove—tall, ancient sequoias, each standing distinct in a dense surrounding forest. While he waited in San Francisco for his family to join him, he was consulted as a landscape architect. The directors of the new Mountain View Cemetery had him design their grounds at Oakland. He had for some time contemplated planning a rural cemetery and became fascinated with the possibilities of the steep, treeless site he had to work with.

During the summer of 1864, he took his whole family camping in the Sierras, making horseback excursions to the Mariposa Big Tree Grove before going on to the fabulous Yosemite Valley for the first time. Its splendid white granite cliffs, almost a mile high and backed by the mighty Sierras, made Olmsted think he was seeing "the greatest glory of nature."[5] Coincidentally, just a month or so before, President Lincoln had signed a bill withdrawing the Yosemite Valley and the Mariposa Big Tree Grove from the public lands and ceding them to the state of California "for public use, resort, and recreation . . . inalienable for all time."[6] Furthermore, Olmsted himself had been designated by the governor of California as one of the commissioners to administer the area for the benefit of all Americans.

The Olmsted family spent several weeks camping on the bank of the Merced River opposite Yosemite Falls and enjoying the scenery. But the climax of Olmsted's vacation that summer was a week's pack trip into the high Sierras with his stepson John and Professor William H. Brewer of Yale, a member of the Geological Survey who had just returned from exploring these mountains. When they reached the 12,500-foot peak, Olmsted claimed the privilege of being the first to climb to the top, naming it Mount Gibbs for his old Sanitary Commission colleague, Wolcott Gibbs, one of the foremost chemists in America.

On his return to the estate, he began to realize that the canal he considered so necessary for a water supply would not be constructed at all. The Mariposa Company was more heavily in debt than he had thought, and he became discouraged about its future. The sad fact was that the gold mines turned out to be on the wrong end of the mother lode. Eventually public confidence in the company dissolved, though Olmsted's personal integrity and the wisdom of his management were unquestioned. A complete panic in Mariposa stock ensued, and the company defaulted on his salary while negotiations with its creditors dragged on. Fortunately, he had invested part of his salary as well as a loan from his father in California stocks that would eventually turn out very well for him. He also inspected oil properties near Santa Cruz for William Ralston, cashier of the Bank of California, who paid him with shares in a promising oil claim.

He found some further landscaping opportunities during this distressing period. His advice was asked on the design of two estates south of San Francisco. The trustees of the College of California, soon to be named Berkeley, picked him to design a campus, residential development, and park across the bay from San Francisco. Finally, supported by the *San Francisco Bulletin*, he became involved in a campaign to provide a large rural park for San Francisco. As a result of his efforts, the Municipal Board asked him to suggest a location and prepare plans for a park.

Olmsted's thoughts, however, were once more turning to the East as he received news from Godkin in June 1865 that the proposed weekly publication, called the *Nation*, was successfully under way. Godkin wanted Olmsted's help on future issues. Olmsted also carefully considered a proposal from Calvert Vaux that they work together on a great public park for Brooklyn, and he decided definitely to return to New York when he and Vaux were reappointed landscape architects to Central Park. He did not completely agree with Vaux on the function of the profession they practiced, regarding himself as much a social engineer as an artist. But he had the highest respect for Vaux's artistic skills and felt a solid foundation existed for further productive collaboration. He could now return to the landscape work he loved, leaving behind an enterprise that was a failure not only financially but socially. While at Mariposa, he had gathered notes for a book about the social tendencies in America in the previous fifty years. He had hoped to transform a transient and semibarbarous frontier population into a stable and civilized community based on mutual interest and respect. His project in social engineering on the frontier was left uninitiated, however, and the book for which his notes were gathered was never finished.

Before Olmsted and his family sailed for New York, he was hard at work on a report for the California legislature concerning the uses appropriate for Yosemite and the Big Tree Grove. Soon after receiving his appointment as a commissioner, he had sent out a survey team to make a topographical map of the area and to plan roads through it according to his instructions. He delivered his report in the Yosemite Valley in August 1865, before an audience of the other commissioners and such distinguished visitors as Samuel Bowles, editor of the *Springfield* (Massachusetts) *Republican*, and the speaker of the United States House of Representatives, Schuyler Colfax. Olmsted's report was the first systematic statement regarding the duty of a democratic government to set aside natural areas of extraordinary beauty for the enjoyment of all the people. It provided the basis for the establishment of all future state and national parks.

Widening Professional Accomplishments

Back once more in New York in November 1865, in the period immediately following the end of the Civil War, Olmsted set to work again in partnership with Vaux. Great professional opportunities lay ahead of him, and he would have a leading role in raising landscape architecture from the level of a trade to that of a fine art. He was in much better health as a result of living in California and was financially independent for the first time in his life. He entered into his duties at Prospect Park with relish. Olmsted and Vaux had an easier job turning the rolling and well-wooded site in Brooklyn into a landscape park than they had had with the rocky spine of Manhattan a few years before. Prospect was shaped under his personal direction, much as Central Park had been, and he tried to relate the park proper to the total life of Brooklyn. He dreamed of using parkways to connect Prospect Park with the south Brooklyn shore and eventually, he hoped, with Central Park. Although this great connected park system linking Brooklyn and New York never became a reality, he was at least able to design two parkways, or boulevards, leading away from Prospect Park that were wider than normal city streets and were amply tree-lined. The Eastern and Ocean parkways, with central pleasure drives for carriages flanked on both sides by pedestrian paths, were to provide pleasant green-belts around the city that would enhance the value of the adjacent land for villa sites.

At the same time that Olmsted was engaged in work on Prospect Park, he also took great interest in the newly founded *Nation*. He spent much spare time at its office doing apparently unpaid work for Godkin as an associate editor. Through the columns of the magazine, he was able to advocate many of his personal interests, such as an international copyright law, equal rights for all citizens, women's suffrage, better training of army officers, and the protection of merchant seamen from cruel and arbitrary ships' officers. During this period, as throughout his career, Olmsted suffered a number of professional disappointments. Some of the Yosemite commissioners on whom he had relied to guide his report through the California legislature suppressed the report for fear that the legislators might authorize funds for Yosemite at the expense of funds for the California Geological Survey. His proposal for a park in San Francisco fell through, only a few parts of his Berkeley plan were carried out, and his advice, sought by the trustees of the Massachusetts and Maine agricultural colleges, was not followed. Nevertheless, such failures did not make him doubt the worth of his ideas. One part of him was a realist who never expected success in all his undertakings. Another part was an optimist who, as an officer of the newly formed American Social Science Association, believed that a social climate was evolving favorable to the promotion of a collective concern for the physical and moral welfare of all Americans.

By 1870 this social climate was inducing city officials and civic leaders in many major cities to consider creating new landscape parks. Clearly an enlightened concern for the public well-being was an important motive, among other motives not so altruistic, in this movement, and Olmsted and Vaux were in the vanguard. They were soon consulted on parks for Chicago, Buffalo, the District of Columbia, Philadelphia, Newark, Albany, and Providence. Their chief professional concerns continued to be Central and Prospect parks, besides the smaller New York and Brooklyn parks and squares assigned to them, but they were building a diversified practice. Olmsted was invited to join a number of professional associations, including the American Institute of Architects. He continued to devote considerable time to the *Nation* and was named head of a committee in charge of exhibits for the Paris Exposition of 1867. Amherst College conferred an honorary master of arts degree on him. He refused the presidency of Iowa's agricultural college and was mentioned as a candidate for the presidency of the College of California.

In 1868 Olmsted and Vaux had their first opportunity to lay out a model suburban village. While in the West, Olmsted had hoped to design a suburb adjacent to the College of California in Berkeley, but his plan was never carried out. Now Emery E. Childs asked the partners to design a residential suburb, to be called Riverside, on the site of a 1,600-acre farm along the Des Plaines River nine miles west of Chicago. In accepting the commission, they indicated that they did not intend simply to create a landscaped park with houses in it. The plan for Riverside would be different from that, combining rural scenery and civilized comfort for commuters to Chicago and their families. And the basic outlines of Riverside were in time developed substantially according to the designers' plan. Well-drained roads and walks were laid out in easy curves to take advantage of the natural configurations of the land along the winding river. Houses were built at least a specified minimum distance from the roads and were approached by private drives. Shade trees were placed not at regular intervals along the roads but irregularly so as to display foliage in varied masses.

Olmsted and Vaux wanted to make Riverside a place that would provide both domestic seclusion and a sense of community for its residents. They appropriated some of the best property for unfenced communal parks and greens like those of country villages, and they even raised the height of the mill dam to make the Des Plaines River wider for boating and skating. The trustees defaulted the following year on their cash payments to the partners, who had to take lots as payment. Even so, Riverside proved to be an early masterpiece in suburban planning, to be followed several years later by another successful suburban community, Tarrytown Heights, New York. There Olmsted and Vaux took a 900-acre tract of picturesque farm land in a region made famous by Washington Irving's *Sketch Book* and created villa sites on it.

As a former resident of Staten Island, Olmsted had long been interested in trying to improve living conditions there and make it a more desirable suburb of New York. He became a member of the Staten Island Improvement Commission, a notable example of what cooperative planning could attempt during the nineteenth century. Enlisting the expert advice of geologists, public health doctors, and sanitary engineers, the Commission drew up a comprehensive fourteen-point plan for the island, taking into account both the natural environment and the future needs of its residents for transportation, housing, parks, and sanitation. Unfortunately, the plan was not adopted. Meanwhile, Olmsted and Vaux continued periodically to have problems handling the affairs of Central Park. They were ignored, though not actually discharged, under the rule of the Tweed Ring beginning in 1868. When the Ring collapsed in 1871, the partners became Landscape Architects Advisory, with authority to accept or reject all structures proposed for the park and with absolute supervision, on Olmsted's insistence, of both the planting and the keeping of the park. At the same time, Frederic E. Church, the Hudson River painter, became a new commissioner at the urging of both partners.

Olmsted joined with Vaux, Church, and a number of other New Yorkers in founding the Metropolitan Museum of Art, and he was a member of its first executive committee. He also became briefly involved in the presidential campaign of 1872 when he was selected, against his will, as the vice-presidential candidate of a dissenting faction of the Liberal Republican party. This faction proved too small to make a politically effective protest, and few people took its nominations seriously. Olmsted found his nomination embarrassing. That same year, 1872, Olmsted and Vaux terminated their partnership. Friction had existed for years between the two men despite their dependence on each other. Among other difficulties, Vaux was resentful that too much credit for Central Park was consistently given Olmsted and too little to himself. Although he knew that Olmsted had taken pains to correct the impression, he could not help blaming his partner for it. Both continued for a time, however, their association with the park, Olmsted as landscape architect with the duties of superintendent and Vaux as consulting landscape architect.

Olmsted's business increased greatly during the 1870s. Besides his continuing responsibility for Central and Prospect parks, he was engaged in planning Riverside Park on the steep upper west side of Manhattan, a main feature of which was the terraced drive, three miles long, overlooking the Hudson River. He also entered into an interesting collaboration with John James Robertson Croes, an experienced civil engineer who had worked for the Croton Water Board. The two men were engaged to design a rapid transit system and a network of roads for the newly annexed Twenty-third and Twenty-fourth wards of New York City, which included upper Manhattan and a part of the Bronx. In what amounted to a marriage of railroad engineering and picturesque park planning, Croes did the rapid transit system, and Olmsted laid out the road system. Breaking away from the mechanical grid pattern of streets characterizing the rest of New York City, Olmsted designed the two wards as a residential suburb with curving roads following the natural topography. But unfortunately, in an unequal struggle with entrenched politicians and real estate speculators, Olmsted and Croes lost their opportunity to create a beautiful suburban district.

Outside New York City, Olmsted continued plans for an extensive park complex that he and Vaux had begun for Buffalo. He began landscaping the grounds around the United States Capitol in Washington, D.C., to create a dignified setting for that massive, formal building. He agreed to plan and supervise the building of Mount Royal Park for the city of Montreal. He was asked by the

Boston commissioners to design a park system there. In addition to these major undertakings, he also did work on the grounds of Amherst and Trinity colleges and planned town squares, summer resort villages, and grounds for private residences.

During these years Olmsted lived with his wife and five children, three of them his deceased brother's children, in a typical New York brownstone he had bought on West Forty-sixth Street in Manhattan. His simply furnished office was located on the ground floor of his home, and his family often helped in his work. For Olmsted, there was little separation between his professional and domestic life. A devoted, ever solicitous father, he took seriously his responsibilities for the children's upbringing. Feeling that his own education had been erratic, he gave considerable personal attention to theirs. The house was full of books of all kinds, and he also encouraged the three boys to develop physical and mechanical skills. When his older stepson, John, finished his studies at the Sheffield Scientific School at Yale, Olmsted brought him into the office. John soon became head draftsman and, in time, a partner.

Olmsted's formal connection with Central Park came to a final end in 1878. Through the years he had experienced many problems in dealing with Andrew Haswell Green and other political figures. When Tammany Hall gained control of the board of commissioners of the park, a majority of the members voted to abolish the office that Olmsted officially headed, the Bureau of Design and Superintendence of the New York Parks, as well as all offices under it. They did add a resolution reappointing Olmsted "Consulting Landscape Architect," to be called in and paid as his services might, on occasion, be required. Their feeling was that Central Park was now completed and no longer required the services of a landscape architect. Although Olmsted's friends, joined by many prominent citizens of both parties and various professions, strongly objected to his dismissal and launched a campaign to have him rehired on the old terms, the board remained adamant: Olmsted was out.

His health broke down during this period. He suffered from chronic insomnia, aggravated now by unusual worry and irritation over Central Park and by frustrations involving his park for Mont-

real. Even a three months' tour of Europe did little for his health
and spirits. Gradually, over the next few years, he decided to leave
New York and settle in Boston. The first summer after his dismissal
from Central Park, he and his family lived in Cambridge, where
he worked on the Arnold Arboretum with Charles Sprague Sargent.
He was also beginning to lay out a park around the Back Bay fens,
the first step in Boston's new park system. In the Boston area he
found congenial company in Godkin, Sargent, Charles Eliot Norton, Asa Gray, Charles Francis Adams, Jr., and Henry Hobson
Richardson.

After this time Olmsted began spending his summers in Brookline, a suburb of Boston that he found increasingly attractive, and
his winters in New York. Finally, in 1883, he made the permanent
move to New England. His final home was the "Clarksted," a dignified, square-fronted old house set on sloping farmland in Brookline. He had to make additions to it that would accommodate his
growing professional needs and at the same time blend in with the
topography of the property. He was soon elected to membership in
the distinguished Saturday Club, which for years had brought together in Boston men of the highest intellectual accomplishment.
Olmsted's friendship and association with Henry Hobson Richardson during these years was especially gratifying to him. Richardson,
already a distinguished architect widely recognized for his work on
Trinity Church in Boston, was probably the most sympathetic and
agreeable architectural collaborator Olmsted ever had. They worked
together on the Staten Island Improvement Commission, the Buffalo
State Hospital, and Niagara Square in Buffalo. They served together on a board to advise the New Capitol Commission on the
New York State Capitol in Albany. In the Boston area, among the
works they did jointly were the Crane Memorial Library at Quincy,
the Converse Memorial Library at Malden, the library, station, and
Ames Memorial Hall at North Easton, Massachusetts, and two
bridges in the Fenway. In addition, their collaboration on a number
of suburban railway stations along the line of the Boston and
Albany Railroad resulted in handsome, well-landscaped structures
that helped meet the needs of rapid suburban growth.

Later Years

During his later years Olmsted's responsibilities continued to be heavy, but he never ceased to be painstaking and exacting in the work he performed for clients from all over the country. He was concerned about the reputation not only of his own firm but of the whole developing profession of landscape architecture as well. He seemed driven to work as hard as he could; indeed, compulsive overwork had been a habit with him since his early Central Park days. Increasingly, well-to-do clients consulted his office about country estates or Newport cottages they wanted designed. Unable to keep up with the demand for his services, he had to rely more on his associates: his stepson John, whom he took into partnership in 1884, and two gifted apprentices, Charles Eliot, son of President Eliot of Harvard, and Henry Sargent Codman, nephew of Charles Sprague Sargent. In time, both Codman and Eliot would also be taken into partnership.

Olmsted felt that the education of public taste was an essential part of a landscape architect's job. He had early recognized the importance of supporting his ideas in writing and had achieved critical acclaim for his multivolume works on the antebellum South. Although he never prepared a systematic treatment of landscape architecture remotely comparable to his classic series on southern society, the principles that guided him in his later career can be found in the scores of individual plans and reports that came from his pen. Unfortunately, as he grew older, the physical and mental labor of writing became more difficult, and what he wrote grew formal, stiff, and sometimes even opaque.

In 1888, with Sargent, Olmsted helped found *Garden and Forest*, a weekly magazine devoted to landscape architecture, forestry, horticulture, and scenic preservation. Despite his busy practice, the common notion still existed that landscape architecture was not really an art at all. For the next ten years the magazine attempted to popularize his belief that it most certainly was. When Sargent became ill at about the time the first issue was to appear, Olmsted stepped in and aided the editor, William A. Stiles, in getting *Garden and*

Forest on its feet. Thereafter, Olmsted's ideas frequently found their way into print, usually indirectly through Stiles, though the attractive publication ultimately proved to be too expensively designed for its own survival. Another problem facing landscape architects was the scarcity of practitioners. At this time the only way of learning the requisite skills in America was through the sort of protracted self-education that Olmsted himself had followed and then apprenticeship in the office of one of the very few practicing landscape architects. Olmsted was eager to encourage promising candidates who asked his advice, and the articles in *Garden and Forest* led a number of them to apply to his office.

Olmsted's last years continued to offer him great opportunities of many kinds. He masterminded a comprehensive park system for Boston that formed a seven-mile green necklace of pleasure drives, parks, and ponds around the city to its culmination in Franklin Park, one of the outstanding rural landscape designs of his career. This park contained six miles of driveways, thirteen of walks, and two of bridle paths. He was also interested in the movement to restore the scenery around Niagara Falls to its early natural condition. He helped devise a plan to protect the falls and organized a campaign to arouse widespread popular support. After a Niagara Falls bill was finally passed by the New York State legislature, Olmsted prepared a design for the state reservation.

In 1886 he was asked to plan the grounds of Stanford University at Palo Alto, California. Senator and Mrs. Leland Stanford decided, after the death of their teenage son, to found a university in his memory. Although Stanford originally wanted his school to have the appearance of a New England college campus, with brick Georgian architecture and broad stretches of green lawns and shade trees, Olmsted explained to him that, because of the semiarid climate of California, it would be advisable to model the campus on the gardens and buildings of the Mediterranean countries instead. The buildings, designed by the Boston firm of Shepley, Rutan, and Coolidge, successor firm to Richardson's after his death, were a combination of California mission architecture, Mediterranean Romanesque, and Richardson's style. The one- or two-story buildings were arranged to form quadrangles, and the necessary shade was provided by formal arcades.

To blend in with this Mediterranean effect, Olmsted took pains to select certain plant materials from Spain and the North African coast that would thrive in Palo Alto through the dry season with a minimum of watering. Through the architecture and landscaping of Stanford University, a radical departure from the usual American academic style of the period, Olmsted revealed his flexible approach to design. He believed that any sound design must be nondoctrinaire, taking into full account not only the client's wishes but the possibilities and limitations of the local environment.

Olmsted's flexibility was further demonstrated in his plan for Biltmore, George Washington Vanderbilt's vast mountain estate near Asheville, North Carolina. When this Vanderbilt, a grandson of the commodore, brought him to Asheville to examine the property in 1888, Vanderbilt had a vague idea of making it into an English deer park. But the soil was poor, Olmsted pointed out, and the topography unsuitable for this purpose. He persuaded Vanderbilt to cultivate the whole estate as a forest, except for a formal park of about 250 acres immediately around the extravagant French chateau that the influential architect Richard Morris Hunt was designing. Vanderbilt, he felt, would derive not only personal enjoyment but the satisfaction of knowing that he was benefiting his country by operating its first large-scale forestry experiment.

The development of the Biltmore estate occurred gradually over a period of years, and in its prime it was the grandest country place in the United States. It became an absorbing interest to Olmsted for the rest of his working life. The relationship between Olmsted and Vanderbilt was informal and unusually pleasant, and Olmsted visited Biltmore two or three times a year, often remaining for weeks at a stretch. Sometimes he traveled to and from Asheville with Vanderbilt by private railway car. Taking delight in the frequent houseguests and long social evenings, he nevertheless spent many hours in the saddle overseeing the complicated operations necessary for a constantly growing estate in the backwoods.

Olmsted's contemporary reputation reached its peak with his contribution to the World's Columbian Exposition, the great Chicago fair of 1893, which marked the four hundredth anniversary of Columbus's discovery of America. In 1890 Olmsted was called upon to lay out the grounds for the fair on a site he himself had selected. Called Jackson Park, the site at that time was really no park at all but merely some 500 acres of swampland on Lake Michigan in Chicago. Twenty years before, as it happened, Olmsted and Calvert Vaux had designed a plan for Jackson Park, but very little of it had been carried out. After reviewing this plan, which featured a chain of interconnecting lagoons, Olmsted decided that it was still generally appropriate. The lagoons would in some instances now become canals. Exhibition buildings could then, he reasoned, be constructed on the raised and extended sandbars, and suitable approaches to these buildings could be provided by land and water.

The Columbian Exposition became famous, among other reasons, for the remarkable collaboration that developed among the country's leading architects, artists, and landscape architects in every phase of the layout and design. During the three years in which the work progressed, Olmsted spent a good deal of time in Chicago conferring with his colleagues. Despite frequent bad health that was aggravated by the traveling he felt compelled to do, he insisted on personally supervising his special interests. He was particularly concerned about the miles of plantings along the shores of the lagoons, the kinds of boats to be used, and the waterfowl that would lend animation to the scene. He was determined to create, above all else, an artistic unity of composition, with the buildings, bridges, shores, boats, and birds all contributing to the coherent effect.

After the successful completion of the Chicago fair grounds, Olmsted was able to devote more attention to the dazzling number of projects his firm continued to take on. During this period the firm was involved with such work as the Frederick Vanderbilt place at Newport, the Lawrenceville School, a new zoological park for Washington, D.C., a large public park development for Rochester, New York, and Downing Park in Newburgh, New York, which Olmsted and Vaux, out of respect for Andrew Jackson Downing's memory, planned without charge. Olmsted conferred with Professor

William R. Ware at Columbia University about the school's new site on Morningside Heights. He was also interested in extending the firm's operations in the South. Besides Biltmore, these included a suburban land development project and the Cotton States Exposition grounds in Atlanta, as well as Cherokee Park in Louisville. Olmsted sometimes worried that the firm had undertaken more jobs throughout the country than it could satisfactorily handle. Now in his seventies, he realized that his partners could not always depend upon him fully on account of his frail health. Still, he had phenomenal drive and was reluctant to have the firm give up attending personally to any part of its far-reaching operations.

The Boston park system was now by far the firm's most important public work. Charles Eliot had led a brilliant campaign, begun in 1890, to bring into being the Boston region's Metropolitan Park Commission. In 1893 he became a partner in Olmsted's firm. That same year the firm was appointed landscape architects to the commission, which was acquiring land in outlying locations so that metropolitan municipalities could combine to preserve their scenic and recreational resources.

In his last productive years Olmsted spent much time and thought grooming his youngest son, Frederick, Jr., to carry on his work. Almost from the birth of the child, Olmsted determined that this son should pursue the profession of landscape architecture and do so with advantages of education he himself had lacked. When the boy was four, Olmsted even changed his name from Henry Perkins to Frederick Law, Jr., so that a Frederick Law Olmsted might continue the firm and the profession after his father's death. Fortunately, the boy's interests were in accord with the father's. Olmsted planned his son's training carefully, giving him the opportunity to work on the Chicago fair for a summer as aide-de-camp to the superintendent of construction. After Frederick was graduated from Harvard, Olmsted set him to work on the Biltmore arboretum for both the prestige and the experience he would gain.

By the spring of 1895, Olmsted realized that his memory was becoming unreliable and that he was losing his grip on professional problems. He told his partners that he could no longer be trusted to play an important part in the firm's business. As his stepson John accompanied him on his last round of visits, Olmsted's senility was becoming more apparent. Plagued by sleeplessness and fits of anxiety, he consoled himself by writing repetitious letters to Frederick at Biltmore. Increasingly he was becoming difficult to handle. Thinking that a change of climate and an enforced rest would be good for him, his doctors sent him to England. His condition did not improve, however, and eventually he was brought home to a year-round cottage that his wife had asked to have built at Deer Isle, Maine. Finally his family committed him to the McLean Hospital at Waverley, Massachusetts. He was settled in a cottage on grounds that, ironically, he had designed years before. Fittingly, Frederick was at his father's bedside at two o'clock on the morning of 28 August 1903 when he died.

Chapter Two

From Gentleman Farmer to Social Critic of the Old South

Gentleman Farmer

One of the amazing facts about Olmsted's career as a landscape architect is that he never deliberately prepared for it at all. His youth and early manhood were characterized by a restless drifting from one enthusiasm to another. Yet, despite the seeming false starts and haphazardness, a coherent pattern emerges in retrospect after all. In his first important career as a farmer, the theories and methods he employed were the same basic ones he was to employ throughout his life. From the beginning he recognized the importance of acquiring scientific knowledge and of analyzing fully the problems at hand before attempting to work out solutions.

Olmsted started out fully convinced of the value of farming as an occupation. It was more to him than simply a way to make a living: it meant a responsible position in the social order. Furthermore, the establishment of model farms of scientific agriculture like the one he developed on Staten Island would, he believed, benefit his fellow countrymen as well as himself. This belief conformed to the philosophy of Andrew Jackson Downing, whom he first met in 1846 in Albany at the office of Luther Tucker, editor of the *Cultivator*, a popular magazine on farming and gardening. Through his books and the magazine he edited, *The Horticulturist*, Downing urged his readers to practice scientific farming, which included improving their livestock breeds, fruits, and vegetables. He also advocated that his readers improve their homes and property for greater convenience and beauty. Downing was probably more influential than any other man in shaping Olmsted's taste and in making him aware of the role of landscape gardening in helping civilize American life.

Then, too, Olmsted found scientific farming personally challenging and appealing. "Rural pursuits," he wrote to his brother, ". . . tend to elevate and enlarge the ideas, for all the proudest aims of Science are involved in them. . . . I believe that our farmers are, and have cause to be, the most contented men in the world."[1] Like Jefferson, whom he admired, Olmsted began by regarding the small independent farm as the cornerstone of democracy. His career as a farmer occurred at a time when the United States was still a predominantly agrarian nation centered on the eastern seaboard. It is not surprising, therefore, that until nearly the age of thirty, he thought of agriculture as an ideal occupation for an enterprising young man. For a time it absorbed most of his energy.

Olmsted probably had an opportunity to hear some of Benjamin Silliman's lectures on geology and scientific agriculture while visiting his brother John at Yale in 1845. His knowledge of the land, however, came primarily through practical experience. After serving as an apprentice on George Geddes's model farm near Syracuse, New York, and struggling to improve the bleak Sachem's Head farm in Connecticut, he was eventually able to apply the latest principles of agricultural science to an imported fruit-tree nursery on the Staten Island farm that his father bought for him in 1848. Putting the soil into full production, Olmsted was soon winning prizes for his pears, wheat, and turnips. He imported English machinery for better results and installed one of the earliest cylindrical drainage tile systems in the United States so that excess water could be removed from the soil. Thus he turned his property into a model of farming and management as well as a beautifully landscaped country seat. In addition, he became secretary of the Richmon County Agricultural Society, founded to help local farmers improve their living conditions and tastes.

Throughout Olmsted's early years nature was a dominant influence, always connected in his mind with the physical beauty of the rural New England landscape and the numerous family trips in which he shared. From these experiences developed a romantic idealism that remained with him to the end of his life. He came to believe that a close association with natural beauty was one of the most necessary elements of human life, providing a psychological balm available nowhere else. It was not unusual that he should have held this belief. Romanticism was in the air during this period, and romanticists saw in unspoiled nature a great force for the renewal of the human spirit bowed down by the pressures of civilization. New England Transcendentalists like Emerson and Thoreau argued that man's essential unity with the divine was reflected in his relation to the natural world around him.

Olmsted was inspired by the cultural flowering of New England, especially the essays and poetry of writers like Emerson, Lowell, and Bryant. He firmly believed, as did the Transcendentalists, in the moral value of nature. In an appeal that he prepared enlisting support for the newly formed Richmond County Agricultural Society on Staten Island in 1849, for example, this belief is manifest. He first enumerated the practical advantages such a society would bring to the island but then, as became characteristic of him, shifted the issue squarely to moral grounds:

We ask you then, Fellow Citizens, one and all, to associate in this Society. . . . We believe it will increase the profit of our labor—enhance the value of our lands—throw a garment of beauty around our homes, and above all, and before all, materially promote Moral and Intellectual Improvement—instructing us in the language of Nature, from whose preaching, while we pursue our grateful labors, we shall learn to receive her Fruits as the bounty, and her Beauty as the manifestation of her Creator.[2]

At about the same time that Olmsted was writing these Emersonian sentiments, he was also recommending Emerson's influential essay *Nature* to his friends in Hartford. Thus Olmsted's romantic

idealism was at the same time a moral and social idealism. He was
sensitive to social problems and felt, all the time that he was working to improve the physical land, a moral and social responsibility
that he was to feel all his life.

Walking Tour Through England

His walking tour through England in 1850 with his brother John
and Charles Loring Brace marks the beginning of a shift in interest
from the rural life to the growth and possibilities of the city. Before
setting out, he attempted to justify his trip in part by writing his
father that he would learn much more about farming by traveling
abroad than by staying at home. But even though the book based
on his travels was titled *Walks and Talks of an American Farmer in
England*, Olmsted devoted considerable time during his tour, and
considerable space in his book, to urban developments. To be sure,
he was delighted with English pastoral scenery, which remained for
him thereafter a yardstick for judging landscapes. But for the first
time he realized the implications of the industrial revolution and the
rapid growth of technology. He became aware of the prodigious
growth of tightly packed industrial towns in England, with more
and more agricultural workers drawn to factories. And he began to
see cities like Liverpool, at which he debarked, emerging as the pro-
totype of the nineteenth-century city.

Olmsted's social idealism was reinforced in England by an increasing concern for the living and working conditions of all classes
of Englishmen. He was especially impressed by what he saw in
Liverpool and devoted more than four chapters in *Walks and Talks*
to it and its new suburb of Birkenhead, the second city in England
(after London) to undertake an extensive program of park development in an effort to improve the lot of its citizens. Most impressive
to him was the new people's park in Birkenhead, planned by a
group of commissioners who, in the progressive spirit of the times,
felt it only right for working men to have their own version of the
landed gentleman's park. Thus the new rural park was consciously
designed so that the congested condition of working men among

factories and docks would be partially offset by an open place offering country scenery. The official opening of Birkenhead Park had occurred in 1847, just three years before Olmsted's visit.

The design of the park astonished the man who would become, within a decade, the designer of the first rural park in the New World: "Indeed, gardening had here reached a perfection that I had never before dreamed of. I cannot undertake to describe the effect of so much taste and skill as had evidently been employed."[3] Olmsted was fascinated by the irregular and deceptively natural design of the park. He was also interested in the technical means by which the design had been achieved, discussing the drainage system, moving of earth, and road surfaces with the head gardener. But equally important to him were the social implications of Birkenhead Park with its completely public ownership: ". . . I was ready to admit that in democratic America there was nothing to be thought of as comparable with this People's Garden. . . . And all this magnificent pleasure ground is entirely, unreservedly, and for ever, the people's own. The poorest British peasant is as free to enjoy it in all its parts as the British queen. More than that, the baker of Birkenhead has the pride of an OWNER in it."[4]

Even at this early stage of his career, then, Olmsted was concerned with the problem of providing civic amenities for the inhabitants of the new industrial cities. He was already becoming a social critic and theorist, recognizing the need for democratic systems of planning that were rational and humane. *Walks and Talks* is of chief interest today not for its account of English farming practices but for its penetrating social observations, expressed with considerable literary skill. Olmsted was concerned with anything he observed that affected human welfare. He had a sociologist's eye for people as members of groups, whether they were Liverpool prostitutes or London factory boys, and a talent for drawing out information in interviews. Another of his remarkable gifts was his memory, which enabled him to reconstruct conversations, even to the point of recording authentic regional dialects.

After his return home to Staten Island, Olmsted visited and commented on another group, this time the North American Phalanx community at Red Bank, New Jersey. Established according to the philosophy of the French utopian socialist Charles Fourier, the Phalanx at Red Bank was part of the communitarian movement that flourished in the pre—Civil War era. Olmsted became interested in the attempt to create model communities away from the growing cities and wrote a long article on "The Phalanstery and Phalansterians," published in the *New York Tribune* in July 1852 under the signature "An American Farmer."

Olmsted discovered at Red Bank that the members spent most of their working hours in farming and market-gardening, making their living almost entirely from the sale of agricultural products. He was surprised to find that they had actually made a profit the previous year and came to believe that a cooperative community would be a great stimulus to the physical and moral improvement of poor farmers. He was somewhat skeptical, however, about the value of such a community for the more educated, feeling that too little attention was given to intellectual pursuits and to those civilizing influences that he thought necessary for a truly democratic society. The Red Bank community, he asserted, was isolated from, and too little concerned about, the outside world. He decided finally that it was not suited to his individual needs, though it might well be suited to others, particularly those obliged to live mainly by manual labor. Still, he expressed gratitude to the members of the Phalanx for the earnestness with which they were carrying on their experiment.

Travels Through the South

The real turning point in Olmsted's attitude toward the agrarian way of life was his travels through the South in the years 1852 to 1854, just prior to the outbreak of the Civil War. By the time Henry J. Raymond, editor of the *New-York Daily Times*, asked him to undertake the tour as a roving correspondent for the paper, Olmsted's *Walks and Talks* had appeared, and his talent for depicting English social life fairly and interestingly was being recognized. In his book Olmsted had noted that the image of America for foreigners was being drawn largely by evangelizing abolitionists. The politically liberal Raymond wanted to present an objective picture of the South and slavery to offset the extreme image drawn by Northern abolitionists like William Lloyd Garrison.

Olmsted had been having recurrent arguments over slavery with his friend Charles Brace, who had become a red-hot abolitionist and had on various occasions brought Garrison and Theodore Parker with him to proselytize at Olmsted's Staten Island farm. Though disliking slavery, Olmsted disliked even more the head-strong fanaticism of extreme abolitionists. He felt that, since in the North there was too little reliable information about slavery as a system of labor, it was impossible to discuss the question constructively. Both he and Brace agreed that the best way to settle their arguments would be for Olmsted, with his enthusiasm for travel and interest in learning about an unfamiliar type of agriculture, to go south and judge conditions at firsthand.

Brace broached the project to Raymond, who was looking for just such a correspondent as Olmsted but had never met him. After only five minutes' discussion, during which Raymond did not even inquire into Olmsted's views on slavery, Olmsted was hired as a special correspondent for the *Times*. The only stipulation was that he should confine his accounts to what he personally observed, and he was urged not to be influenced by the paper's editorial position on slavery.

Few men could have been so little inclined to rely on previously formed opinions as Olmsted was as he set out on his assignment in December 1852. To an extraordinary degree he had avoided the emotions that had for so long inflamed the thinking of both Northerners and Southerners on the issue of slavery, and he was therefore not tempted to engage in special pleading. A national controversy had recently arisen over Harriet Beecher Stowe's sensational portrait of slavery in *Uncle Tom's Cabin*, which appeared serially in 1851–52. And readers were becoming used to the reports pouring forth from the pens of such native and foreign travelers in the South as Fanny Kemble, the actress, Charles Dickens, and Harriet Martineau—reports usually unfavorable to slavery.

As a believer in democracy, Olmsted could not approve of slavery in principle, but he recognized the clear constitutional right of the Southern states to continue the institution of slavery as it existed. In fact, he regarded abolition as no more immediately practicable than the abolition of penitentiaries or hospitals. He believed that a long educational process would be required to fit slaves for freedom. Immediate freedom would cast them, without preparation, on their own resources and would create worse problems than it solved. He tended to view slavery per se as an "unfortunate circumstance for which the people of the South were in no wise to blame."[5]

Olmsted visited the eastern sections of Virginia, the Carolinas, and Georgia as far south as Savannah. Then he pushed westward through central Georgia and Alabama, taking the steamer from Mobile to New Orleans. He spent most of his time in the hill country, studying living conditions wherever he went. His return home was through the interior of the slaveholding South by way of Vicksburg, Memphis, and then along the eastern base of the Appalachians through upper Mississippi, Alabama, Georgia, the Carolinas, and Virginia. The entire journey took almost four months. Henry Raymond was so pleased with Olmsted's accounts, signed "Yeoman" to suggest a small Yankee farmer traveling without fanfare through the South, that he soon commissioned his correspondent to make a trip to a different part of the South. This time Olmsted had as a companion his brother John, whose tuberculosis, it was hoped, would be improved by a winter spent on horseback in the open air.

Heading for Texas, the two brothers left in November 1853 by rail for Wheeling on the Ohio River. They continued by steamboat, stage, and rail to Nashville and then proceeded to New Orleans. In mid-December at Natchitoches, Louisiana, on the Red River near the Texas border, they bought horses and supplies for a saddle trip through the ranching and farming country of Texas, passing through Austin on their way to San Antonio. They had originally planned to visit California as well as Texas, but Indian outbreaks made this part of the trip impossible so they set out instead on a short jaunt into northern Mexico. By May 1854 the brothers were back in New Orleans, where they parted company. Since John's health was not improved, he took the steamer from New Orleans to New York. Frederick took the opportunity to round out his knowledge of the South and set off alone on horseback for the East. He headed across central Mississippi and through the Appalachian highlands to Richmond, from which he returned to New York by steamer. This third expedition, lasting from May to August, covered the infrequently visited southern hill country, or what Olmsted called the back country. Though he apparently made this final trek on his own initiative, he eventually published ten unsigned articles about it in the *New York Herald*, a new medium for him.

Social Critic of the Old South

Altogether, Olmsted spent about fourteen months traveling from one end of the South to the other, and eventually he expanded and published the newspaper accounts that first appeared in the *Times* and *Herald* as three separate volumes that constitute a kind of trilogy: *A Journey in the Seaboard Slave States* (1856); *A Journey Through Texas, or, A Saddle-Trip on the Southwestern Frontier* (1857); and *A Journey in the Back Country* (1860). Collectively, these works, dealing with all aspects of southern culture, present a uniquely honest and realistic picture of the pre–Civil War South. Written in the fateful decade between the Compromise of 1850 and Lincoln's election as president, they present the definitive critique of the plantation society that time has glamorized with romantic legend.

Alexis de Tocqueville, traveling in the United States in the 1830s, had maintained that almost all the differences observable between Americans in the North and South at that time originated in slavery.[6] Olmsted, after a much more careful examination of conditions twenty years later, came to a similar conclusion. He did not make the mistake of considering the entire South as a homogeneous economic and social area. But though well aware of differences, he found the common denominator to be the practice of slavery, which made the South distinct from the rest of the United States and from most of the Western world.

Olmsted discovered, first, that slave labor was an exasperating inconvenience to plantation owners and managers. Then, with his training as a scientific farmer to guide him, he concluded that the most serious defect of the system was that this type of labor typically yielded a very low level of productivity. Since it was costlier than free labor, it constituted a hindrance to southern progress that he felt was sufficient in itself to account for the disparity between the prosperity of North and South. As a general rule, he found that slaves worked slowly and carelessly, taking two to four times as long to perform a given task as an Irish or German hired hand. He rejected, however, the theory that it was the hot climate rather than the slave system that accounted for the South's backwardness. He noted that the most prosperous civilizations of antiquity had a climate warmer than that of Virginia and also that many southern whites worked on farms producing cotton and other crops.

Olmsted found that slaves could not be trusted with complicated tools or with jobs requiring skill and judgment. They needed close supervision. He did not argue that slave labor was always necessarily unprofitable since he visited some plantations that did operate at a profit, at least when the price of their cotton, rice, or sugar was high. But he contended that these profitable plantations would have shown an even greater profit if free labor had been employed. Furthermore, he found that slavery was a boon only to those at the very top of the southern economic pyramid—for just the upper two percent of the slaveholders.

Olmsted's investigation of the economic implications of slavery inevitably led to its moral aspects. Although he was frequently impressed with the poor workmanship and unreliability of the slaves, he attributed these qualities not to the slaves' racial or native inferiority but to their enslaved condition, which as a rule deprived them of incentive. He remarked a number of times on slaves who, offered responsibility and incentive, worked efficiently and developed skills that compared favorably with those of free white work-men. The problem, therefore, lay not in the black man himself but in his slave status. To treat a human being as a slave was to deprive him of the attributes that distinguish a man from a beast, and this treatment was, to Olmsted, immoral.

He found the physical treatment of slaves better than he had expected. Almost everywhere in the South they were provided with adequate food, clothing, and shelter. Although they were subject to frequent and harsh discipline, and were even occasionally killed through cruel punishment, still he felt that they were not mistreated as often as sailors were by careless and brutal masters. In general, he discovered that slave owners treated their slaves with considerable indulgence, even though it was an indulgence stemming from a feeling of complete superiority. The real problem, however, was that the slaves were, on the whole, deliberately held back mentally and morally. Kept in a state of almost primitive superstition, they were not encouraged to read, to think for themselves, or to provide for the future. And while house servants might be improved by association with a cultivated family, the field hands were usually deprived of civilizing influences.

In addition to the deplorable effects of slavery upon the blacks, Olmsted also found it dehumanizing the whites in southern society. He came to realize that no man can have absolute power over others without its corrupting his sense of justice and humanity. While traveling in eastern Tennessee, Olmsted commented on the particularly violent reaction of a newspaper editor, who was also a Methodist preacher, to the public burning of a slave. The editor had wanted to have the slave tortured in public as well as burned: "We unhesitatingly affirm that the punishment was unequal to the crime. Had we been there, we should have taken a part, and even suggested the pinching of pieces out of him with red-hot pincers—the cutting off of a limb at a time, and then burning them all in a heap."[7] Olmsted concluded that such savage behavior was conditioned by the social system: "To follow the usual customs of civilization elsewhere would not be felt safe. . . . To act in a spirit of cruel, inconsiderate, illegal, violent, and pitiless vengeance must be permitted, must be countenanced, must be defended by the most conservative, as a 'means of absolute, necessary self-defense.' "[8]

Then, too, the institution of slavery tended to stultify the southern mind, imposing a strict censorship on freedom of the press and of speech regarding slavery and religion. Olmsted found southerners frequently reluctant to talk about slavery, and he discovered a kind of intellectual blockade imposed on antislavery magazines and newspapers from the North. Moreover, where the laborer lacked respect, labor necessarily did also. The majority of southern whites were not slaveholders, and a great number of them were lazy and unambitious. In fact, Olmsted found that white southern labor was even less efficient than slave labor, accomplishing on the average only about two-thirds as much as slaves. The aversion to manual labor arose from the fact that to work industriously and steadily, especially under directions from others, was regarded by the whites as the lot of slaves—whence came the southern expression "to work like a nigger." Even conscientious white workmen had little incentive to produce where work was habitually performed badly.

Olmsted became convinced that the primitive manner of living in much of the South—the lack of conveniences, the wretched transportation, the addiction to violence, the scarcity of newspapers, schools, churches, lyceums, and community services—did not ultimately stem from frontier conditions. In the free states of the North, pioneer life was usually a transitional stage, a spur to improvement, something to be left behind. In the slave states, however, the primitive order of existence tended to be permanent. In the rural South, from Virginia to Texas, Olmsted hardly ever saw a volume of Shakespeare, a sheet of music, or a good art engraving. Random conversation along the way suggested, moreover, that the level of general information was not much better. He could not avoid the conclusion that slavery was prolonging the barbarism that usually belongs only to a frontier. He cited as prime evidence the oldest of the slave states, Virginia, where an essentially stagnant, even retrogressive society still existed in places after more than two centuries.

Probably no more effective book deglamorizing the Old South

has ever been written than Olmsted's *A Journey in the Back Country*. His extensive descriptions of the quaint and primitive highlanders of the southern Appalachians, while falling short of the stark naturalism of Caldwell's *Tobacco Road* or Faulkner's *Sanctuary*, make a devastating impact, portraying these Southerners largely as tragic victims of a slave economy.

Olmsted's social criticism reveals a man fundamentally conservative by nature. The convictions he reached during the 1850s did not make him denunciatory, nor did they lead him to withhold from his readers facts that did not document his views. With great care, he noted exceptions unfavorable to his arguments. And even as late as 1860 his views continued to be moderate in a political climate of accelerating crisis. Although he detested slavery in the abstract, he still felt that the whites were caught in a historical trap and that, everything considered, the subjection of the blacks in the South to the whites was "justifiable and necessary."[9]

In accordance with this belief, Olmsted continued to criticize the provocative outbursts of the Northern abolitionists, whose high moral tone ignored what he considered the practical difficulties of emancipation. He also condemned their contempt for Southerners as individuals and their willingness to jeopardize for their cause the very survival of the Union. In his opinion, these abolitionists were as wrongheaded as those at the other end of the spectrum who staunchly defended slavery. "The extremists of the South," he declared, "esteem their opponents as madmen, or robbers," while "the extremists of the North esteem the slave-holders as robbers and tyrants, willfully and malevolently oppressive and cruel."[10]

Travels in Western Texas

During their travels in western Texas, Olmsted and his brother were surprised and delighted to encounter, between Austin and San Antonio, German settlements that reminded them of their walking tour through the Rhine Valley several years before. Here was an oasis of civilization in the midst of the ignorance and brutishness perpetuated by a slave economy. Here were German people on the

American frontier who rejected slavery, Olmsted reported to the
Times, worked better and cheaper than slaves, and by example and
influence were "uprooting the system more than all the ranting
attacks of Abolitionists for the last twenty years."[11] The neat, close-
knit little town of New Braunfels, settled by poor but cultivated
emigrants from repression in central Europe, all but overwhelmed
the Olmsteds, who were treated as honored guests for some weeks.
John Olmsted was even strongly tempted to send for his family and
settle permanently in the community.

An interesting possibility presented itself at this historical moment. Since Texas, as admitted to the Union in 1845, exceeded in
area New England, the Middle Atlantic states, Maryland, Virginia,
and Kentucky combined, Congress had provided that, as the population increased, the state might be broken up into as many as five
smaller states. Western Texas was one candidate for statehood, and
it was possible therefore that this area might in time enter the
Union as a free state by the choice of its inhabitants.

One of the Germans whom Olmsted most admired was Dr. Adolf
Douai, editor of the *San Antonio Zeitung,* a German-language
newspaper that was the second largest of the papers then published
in Texas. Douai was leader of the movement to make western Texas
into a free state. When some of the paper's stockholders, fearful of
antagonizing the local slaveowners, tried to restrain him, he appealed in September 1854 to the Olmsted brothers, then back in
New York, for a loan to enable him to buy the *Zeitung* and continue publishing on his own. The Olmsteds quickly gathered funds
from Charles Brace, Henry Ward Beecher, and other antislavery
sympathizers. They helped Douai obtain English type so that he
could reach Americans as well as Germans, and drummed up sub-
scribers among their friends.

Furthermore, Olmsted wrote articles for the *Zeitung* and persuaded Henry Raymond of the *Times* to publish editorials encouraging northern emigration to western Texas. For political reasons,
these pieces intentionally avoided the slavery issue and emphasized
the economic advantages of the region instead. Douai, however,

eventually found the local opposition too powerful and was forced in 1856 to sell his paper.

During the time that Olmsted was supporting the Texas Free-Soilers in their campaign, he quietly became involved in a similar campaign to keep slavery out of Kansas. The dispute over this area, growing out of the passage of the Kansas-Nebraska Act in 1854, was much more prominent nationally and had become violent. The Kansas Free-Soilers sent an agent east to collect money and buy arms. Olmsted, with the assistance of Horace Greeley of the *Tribune*, succeeded in providing them with a twelve-pound brass howitzer that he found in the New York State Arsenal. The howitzer arrived in Kansas just as the Free-Soilers and the proslavery forces were on the brink of warfare. Negotiations averted bloodshed for the moment, and the howitzer was retired, anticlimactically, to a cellar in Lawrence, Kansas.

But Olmsted's deeper concern seems to have remained with western Texas, possibly because he felt that northerners were already sufficiently disturbed over "Bleeding Kansas." His book *A Journey Through Texas* did not directly propagandize for immigration to the Lone Star state but contained a great deal to promote interest in it. He hoped that settlers would be drawn by the book from Kansas and from the northern states. Though the prospect of making a free state out of western Texas had now faded, he nevertheless believed that the superior efficiency of free labor in the production of cotton would lead to the curtailment or even abandonment of slave labor. Hearing that some of the Kansas Free-Soilers were hoping to move on to western Texas, he offered the New England Emigrant Aid Society a hundred copies of his book at cost to distribute among them. He gave other copies to leading antislavery men like Theodore Parker and John Greenleaf Whittier, and even circulated excerpts from the work to New England newspaper editors.[12]

Olmsted considered the possibility of further immigration from Germany, where *A Journey Through Texas* came out in translation in 1857, but he expended even greater effort in encouraging immigration from England, where factories were dependent on the southern cotton crop and where manufacturers were alarmed by impending shortages. He contended that free English laborers, in collaboration with the Germans, could grow cheaper and better cotton than that which could be purchased from the slave plantations. Unfortunately, Olmsted's scheme came to nothing. His appeals to the recently formed English cotton supply associations were rejected on the grounds that English colonists going to western Texas to form free-labor communities would be exposed to border ruffianism like that in turbulent Kansas. And if England were to encourage any such migration, she would create the impression that she was meddling in the internal affairs of the United States.

Olmsted continued to draw a careful distinction between federal interference with slavery as a preexisting institution in the South and its extension to new soil. He still looked upon slavery where it was already rooted as a misfortune that might require centuries to be completely eradicated. And he opposed instant emancipation by federal edict, not only on constitutional grounds but also because he doubted whether it would accomplish what was expected: "An extraction of the bullet does not at once remedy the injury of a gun-shot wound; it sometimes aggravates it."[13]

His own long-range solution was gradual emancipation by action of the slave owners themselves. This solution he regarded as not improbable, once the owners came to realize the economic drawbacks of the old system. As steps toward the goal, an owner would systematically promote habits of self-reliance among his slaves and permit them eventually to buy their freedom by accumulating financial credits for work accomplished. Olmsted did not expect startling results: "I do not suppose that in one generation or two the effects of centuries of barbarism and slavery are to be extinguished. I do not think negroes are ever to become Teutons or Celts, but I do suppose that negroes may become thoroughly civilized, thoroughly independent individuals, and thus of tenfold more value in the commonwealth than they are."[14] This doctrine of gradual and compensated emancipation was very different from that of the abolitionists, who held that freedom was a God-given right and that the slaveholding class, having exploited the blacks for many generations, deserved no further compensation of any kind. Olmsted took what he considered a less abstract, more pragmatic approach. As much as he desired the freedom of the slaves, he did not wish to bring about the utter destruction of the white owners. He remained concerned with the practical substitution of one system of labor for another and with the importance of carefully educating the slaves for freedom.

All three volumes of Olmsted's trilogy on the South won considerable critical acclaim in the North, where even such abolitionists as William Lloyd Garrison and Theodore Parker, who disliked his conciliatory and gradualist tone, praised his depiction of southern society. Charles Eliot Norton called the books the "most important contributions to an exact acquaintance with the conditions and results of slavery in this country that have ever been published. They have permanent value, and will be chief material for our social history whenever it is written." English reviews were, in general, equally favorable. Dickens, who had traveled in the South, asserted that Olmsted had reported the situation accurately. And Charles Darwin called *Back Country* "an admirable picture of man and society in the Southern States."[15] Only in the South did most newspapers and magazines find Olmsted grossly unfair.

The Cotton Kingdom

Much sooner than he had expected, the secession of slave states began after Lincoln's election in the autumn of 1860. Unlike many other Northerners, Olmsted had no doubts as to what course the federal government should follow in the emergency. He had deep nationalistic feelings and took his stand unqualifiedly with the Union—that Union that he had so painstakingly tried to hold together by peaceful means. Although the new administration had not yet taken office, he wrote Charles Brace in December that "my mind is made up for a fight. The sooner we get used to the idea, the better, I think."[16]

Olmsted gave special thought to how he might serve his country. He was disqualified from active military service because he had badly injured his leg in a carriage accident the previous summer. Was there any way now in which he could use his firsthand knowledge of slavery and its practices to strengthen the national cause? At this moment Sampson Low, Son and Company of London, the firm that had managed the English sales of his three books, made an attractive proposition. It invited him to condense his writings into a single work for English readers. Olmsted had long been concerned about the English attitude toward the slavery issue and keenly realized its importance in the present crisis. He knew that influential Britons favored the South and that the secessionists counted on the British ministry's support in the event of war with the North. Under these circumstances he was eager to do what he could to enlist English support for the Union.

Although the Sampson Low proposal involved no remuneration for Olmsted personally, the firm promised to supply the book plates free for an American edition. After his New York publishers, Mason Brothers, offered him a royalty of 12.5 percent, he accepted the entire arrangement. Since he was by this time heavily involved in the creation of Central Park, he asked the journalist Daniel Reeves Goodloe to help with the revisions in return for half the royalties from Mason Brothers. Goodloe, editor of the *National Era*, a moderate antislavery paper, was a natural choice because of his authoritative writings on the economics of slavery, and he agreed to the offer at once.

The two men had to work quickly, for the rapid march of events —the beginning of the war at Fort Sumter followed by England's recognition of the belligerent status of the rebels—dictated as soon a publication date as possible. Olmsted decided to prepare a brand-new, substantial introduction called "The Present Crisis" to bring the work completely up to date. By the middle of June 1861 the finished manuscript was on its way to England. When it was published in the fall, it bore the title *The Cotton Kingdom: A Traveller's Observations on Cotton and Slavery in the American Slave States*. Olmsted dedicated the new edition to John Stuart Mill, champion of "moral and political freedom" in England and a good supporter of the northern cause. The title was a play on Senator

James H. Hammond's fire-eating speech of 1858 vaunting King Cotton, from which Olmsted quoted in his introduction. The cotton monopoly, Olmsted insisted, was far from being a pillar of strength to the South. It was, instead, a source of weakness despite the large profits accruing to a few planters. Thus King Cotton was, ironically, a cruel and ruinous monarch.

With the North and South now at war, Olmsted's cherished hope of a voluntary and gradual emancipation of the slaves vanished. His introduction to *The Cotton Kingdom* revealed how far he had come since his first series of articles in the *Times* almost nine years before. Gone were the conciliatory statements previously expressed. In their place was his carefully reasoned conviction that the North could make no peace with the South as a separate power. One or the other had to be vanquished and compelled to accept the labor system of the victor: "The instant effect of the first *shotted*-gun that was fired"[17] at Fort Sumter proved that slavery must crush or be crushed. This was war to the finish. The South "must come under the yoke of freedom, not to work for us, but to work with us, on equal terms, as a free people."[18]

The Cotton Kingdom sold well both in England and in the United States. It would be impossible to measure its exact effect on opinion in England, the book being one of a great many factors in Anglo-American relations during the Civil War. It enraged the ultra-Tory *Saturday Review*, yet through reviews and articles in a number of British publications, Olmsted's ideas reached a wide public. In addition, they influenced men who were themselves greatly influential, among them John Stuart Mill and the Irish economist John Elliot Cairnes. Mill wrote an article in which he acknowledged his reliance on "the calm and dispassionate Mr. Olmsted." Mill went on to denounce the southern cause as an effort to perpetuate a villainous institution. Denying the legality of secession, he warned that in case of a southern victory, England would have to fight the Confederacy within five years.[19]

Cairnes, one of the outstanding economists of the mid-nineteenth century, quoted repeatedly from Olmsted in his book *The Slave Power: Being an Attempt to Explain the Real Issues Involved in the American Contest,* published in London in 1862. His polemical treatise was a powerful indictment of the southern system on economic grounds. Alarmed at the sympathy among certain Englishmen for the southern cause, Cairnes attempted to demonstrate that both morality and economic self-interest dictated that Great Britain should refrain from intervening in the Civil War on behalf of the Confederacy. His main arguments were clearly derived from Olmsted.

In the United States *The Cotton Kingdom* was well received. James Russell Lowell wrote to Olmsted that he was particularly impressed with the "compactness and quiet power" of the new introduction. "I have learned more about the South from your books," he continued, "than from all others put together, and I valued them the more that an American who can be patient and accurate is so rare a phenomenon."[20]

In the midst of his exacting duties as chief executive officer of the United States Sanitary Commission, Olmsted pondered the fate of the blacks in the South. He considered "savage" his friend Charles Brace's suggestion that the slaves be stirred up to rise against their masters.[21] The slaves, he felt, ought to be used, but in an orderly way. In a letter to the *New York Times* published in December 1861, he called on the federal government to seize and fortify strategic points to which slaves could escape and thus help demoralize the South. He also proposed arming the slaves, arguing that to subject them to military discipline would reduce rather than increase the danger of servile insurrection.[22] No official action was taken, however, upon his suggestions, nor was any comprehensive policy yet formulated for dealing with contrabands, the slaves who escaped to the Union lines. He feared that the slaves would be emancipated long before the government could deal with them decently. He had long held that abrupt emancipation would only subject them, untrained to take care of themselves, to cruel hardship.

Olmsted's next proposal urged federal authorities to provide constructive employment for newly freed blacks in southern districts occupied by northern troops. After the Union forces captured the sea islands in Port Royal Sound off the coast of South Carolina, he wanted to show that the blacks would be willing to work for wages and would work effectively. He was still preoccupied with attempting to prove to the South the economic mistake of slavery, while at the same time desiring to train the blacks in a few fundamental duties of free men.

Olmsted helped Senator Lafayette Foster of Connecticut draw up a bill outlining a plan of management for contrabands. The bill was finally passed in the United States Senate but for political reasons never passed in the House. Instead, a special agent and a contingent of missionaries and teachers sponsored by several private philanthropic societies were sent to the Port Royal plantations. At one point Olmsted himself was asked to take over the entire management of these plantations, including the blacks, but somehow the project collapsed. He, however, was philosophical about the failure of his appointment and did not consider his three months of lobbying wasted since he had been able to impress his views on the members of the philanthropic societies. And after Lincoln issued the Emancipation Proclamation, Olmsted participated actively in the discussions that led Congress to create the Bureau for the Relief of Freedmen and Refugees.

Continued Interest in the South

His interest in the South continued throughout the rest of his life. A quarter of a century later, he took a retrospective look at the social and economic changes that had occurred there. After the Civil War he had felt that the great mass of freedmen were "as yet ludicrously unfitted to be trusted with the ballot." Nevertheless, he had believed that, unless suffrage for the blacks was granted, danger existed of a revival of the old sectional conflict and even of reenslavement. He still hoped that the southern states would enact an effective literacy test for voting and urged the use of machinery to make it apply equally to both races. But despite these problems, he admitted that the blacks were doing a great deal better as freedmen than he had ever expected.[23]

In the light of Olmsted's later illustrious career as a landscape architect and urban planner, it is easy to lose sight of his accomplishments as a social and economic critic of the South. Sometimes it almost seems as if he were two different men. Yet even if he had done nothing memorable after the Civil War, he would still be important for his far-reaching impact before and during the war. In addition, he has had a profound effect on social and economic history down to the present, having been instrumental in shaping the traditional interpretation of the slave economy. Almost every historian who has dealt with the Old South has paid tribute to Olmsted's skillfulness and scrupulousness as an observer. W. E. B. DuBois, Ulrich B. Phillips, Richard Hofstadter, Clement Eaton, John Hope Franklin, and Eugene D. Genovese are only some of the historians of North and South alike whose conceptions of slavery he has influenced.

Olmsted has frequently been praised for his ability to see both sides of the issues he confronted in the South. In "The Crack-Up" F. Scott Fitzgerald has suggested that "the test of a first-rate intelligence is the ability to hold two opposed ideas in the mind at the same time, and still retain the ability to function."[24] Olmsted would seem amply to have met these specifications. While forthrightly expressing his own judgments, he at the same time carefully presented detailed evidence from which his readers might draw their own conclusions. As he stated in *A Journey in the Back Country*, "my conscious first purpose has been to obtain and report facts of ordinary life at the South, not to supply arguments."[25] His frequently allowing the Southerners to speak for themselves accounts, in part, for the bulkiness of his works.

Even those historians who have questioned some of Olmsted's inferences have tended to trust his reporting of facts. Recently, however, a challenge to his reliability has been issued by revisionist historians Robert William Fogel and Stanley L. Engerman in their book *Time on the Cross: The Economics of American Negro Slavery*, published in 1974. Fogel and Engerman contend that Olmsted shared the racial biases of his time, biases based upon racial theories that came into prominence during the first half of the nineteenth century and were embraced by northerners as well as southerners, by critics of slavery as well as its defenders. These theories asserted that blacks and whites were of different species, or at least that blacks were an inferior variety of the human species. Thus Fogel and Engerman proceed to argue that, partly because of these racial biases, Olmsted grossly underestimated the efficiency and dependability of slave labor and helped to brand the blacks with the stereotype of laziness, incompetence, and unreliability that has handicapped them down to the present. If the Fogel and Engerman interpretation is correct, on the other hand, black slave labor was far more productive than the free white labor of the antebellum South.[26]

Whatever the verdict of future historians as to the validity of this revisionist interpretation, Olmsted was obviously well ahead of his time not only in his sympathy for blacks but in his optimism about their potentiality for advancement in a favorable environment. Whether he is considered an unconscious racist or not, he was clearly paternalistic toward the blacks. And yet, in any evaluation of the man, his relative enlightenment ought certainly to deserve more emphasis than any bias.

Olmsted's works on the South deserve to be read quite apart from the value of his observations on the slave economy. He managed somehow to capture the whole richness of southern life. In his book *Patriotic Gore*, Edmund Wilson, though noting that Olmsted's syntax is sometimes awkward, has remarked on the traveler's vivid ear for the southern accent and language: "He talked to everybody and he sized up everything, and he wrote it all down."[27] His books contain passages of American frontier humor that relate him to the tradition of Augustus B. Longstreet and Mark Twain. They also contain descriptive rhapsodies revealing his delight in the beauty of the southern landscape.

In many ways Olmsted came to admire the wealthy southern gentlemen of the plantation aristocracy, finding them dignified, chivalrous, and genial. In fact, he discovered "less vulgar display, and more intrinsic elegance, and habitual refinement in the best society of South Carolina, than in any distinct class" of the North.[28] The dreaming side of Olmsted's nature could appreciate the ability of southern gentlemen to enjoy life in and for itself. Yet, for all his praise of the South Carolina gentry, the puritanical, disciplined side of his nature felt that they had not been sufficiently concerned with progress. They had done little "for the advancement of learning and science, and there have been fewer valuable inventions and discoveries, or designs in art, or literary compositions of a high rank," than in "any community of equal numbers and wealth, probably in the world."[29] Furthermore, Olmsted noted that the sense of honor of these southern aristocrats was dictated by conventional, external standards rather than by an enlightened conscience that he considered the "noblest endowment of man." This enlightened conscience he found strongly developed in more Northerners than Southerners.[30]

Olmsted's travels through the South considerably strengthened his belief in democracy. He admitted the lack of culture prevalent among the northern working classes, but he could not accept the southern view that the democracy of northern society was responsible for this deficiency. On the contrary, he argued, a greater commitment to democratic values would in time remedy the situation. He understood democracy to mean something more than the mere exercise of the political process. Politics ought not to be a means of protecting the interest of the rich and powerful but a way of helping the majority to advance. Its real goal was social justice.

In one of Olmsted's concluding articles during his first southern trip for the *Times*, he argued that the government had a greater responsibility to its citizens than the protection of laissez-faire capitalism. It ought to educate the "aesthetic faculties" of its citizens as well as encourage the useful arts. Government should support "public parks and gardens, galleries of art and instruction in art, music, athletic sports and healthful recreations, and other means of cultivating taste and lessening the excessive materialism of purpose in which we are, as a people, so cursedly absorbed."[31] A democratic government had a significant role to play, therefore, in elevating the working classes, which would benefit from association with the more cultivated elements of society in such activities as he outlined.

Just as Olmsted's experiences in the South made him realize the values of democracy, so they served to commit him to the social improvement of the city. In meeting southern leaders, he listened to them defend their culture by citing the vulgarity inherent in the commercialism of northern cities. Southern apologists like William Harper and James D. B. De Bow argued that the commercial city was contrary to the Anglo-Saxon tradition of agrarianism. Northern cities, they pointed out, contained many poor immigrants morally degraded by the very nature of urban life. Thus the North had spawned a much higher rate of drunkenness, prostitution, and crime than the South, with its predominantly rural society based on a well-controlled labor force of slaves. Olmsted acknowledged that the commercial North had yet to create a society truly worthy of a democracy. But he rejected the idea that the densely populated cities need remain as they were. And his experience in the South had taught him that a "purely agrarian economy built on the isolated farm or plantation could never meet the increasingly complex demands" of the nation.[32]

Even before the publication of his third volume on the Old South, Olmsted was busy superintending his first important urban project, the construction of Central Park in New York City. Here he could demonstrate the cultural awareness of a free urban society. He well knew William Harper's often-quoted statement that history proved that only slave societies were capable of creating architecture of lasting greatness. "Let it be remembered," wrote Harper, "that all the great and enduring monuments of human art and industry—the wonders of Egypt—the everlasting works of Rome—were created by the labor of slaves."[33] Central Park might be considered Olmsted's refutation of Harper. It was, he wrote to his friend Parke Godwin, "a democratic development of the highest significance and on the success of which . . . much of the progress of art and aesthetic culture in this country is dependent."[34]

Chapter Three

The New York City Parks

Beginnings of Central Park

In retrospect it is easy to say that Frederick Law Olmsted was the ideal man to superintend the landscaping of Central Park. In a variety of ways he had prepared himself for this undertaking that was to launch him on his great subsequent career as the father of American landscape architecture. Yet his magnificent opportunity came to him quite by chance at a time when he was preoccupied by serious business and personal problems. Dix and Edwards, the publishing firm in which he had invested, had just gone bankrupt, and he had lost a good deal of money. He was also trying hard to sell his farm on Staten Island and was frustrated by his lack of success. And, finally, he was heartbroken over the slow death from tuberculosis of his brother John.

The opportunity presented itself in August 1857 while Olmsted was finishing his book *A Journey in the Back Country* at a seaside inn outside New Haven, Connecticut. At tea one day, he happened to sit next to Charles W. Elliott, one of the eleven commissioners recently appointed to take over the immense new landscaping project in the middle of Manhattan. Elliott mentioned that preliminary clearing had already begun and that a superintendent would soon be appointed to direct the labor force building the park and to enforce the rules governing park use. He suggested that Olmsted apply for the job. Until the suggestion was made, the possibility of taking such a job had never occurred to Olmsted, but he immediately resolved to try. "Nothing interested me in London like the parks," he declared, "and yet I thought a great deal more might be made of them."[1] By the next day he was in New York collecting signatures for a petition to the Central Park Commission.

In 1857 not a single large, rural public park existed in any city in the United States. When, six years before, the New York State legislature passed what has come to be known as the First Park Act, a historic milestone was reached in setting aside land to be developed for public enjoyment and recreation. To be sure, urban open spaces had existed for centuries, but ownership usually rested in the hands of the ruling classes. The royal parks of London, for example, which were originally the hunting preserves and gardens of royalty, had gradually been opened to public use, but they remained the property of the crown. On his trip to England in 1850, Olmsted had grasped the significance of the public ownership of Birkenhead Park when he made his enthusiastic visit there. Prior to the creation of this park (and the slightly older Victoria Park in East London) during the reform-conscious 1830s and 1840s, no record exists of any sizable outdoor recreational space on land acquired and owned by the people themselves.

In the Western hemisphere, open spaces developed in American cities as they grew. Cities like Savannah and Philadelphia had their distinctive town squares, and Major Pierre L'Enfant's plan for the new federal city of Washington provided for generous open spaces at the crossings of the radiating avenues. But generally these spaces were accidental results of whatever street patterns occurred in the cities. Even though New York had its Battery and Bowling Green at the lower tip of Manhattan, as well as a so-called park at City Hall a little farther north, these were inadequate to meet the city's growing need for recreational facilities. To fill the gap, rural cemeteries served for a while during the early nineteenth century as places of public recreation. The first of these, Mount Auburn Cemetery, was established in Cambridge, Massachusetts, in 1831 by a Boston physician and botanist who believed that the traditional churchyard burial ground constituted a danger to public health. Mount Auburn soon became popular as a place for quiet walks and even family picnics, and other cemeteries of the same kind sprang up in imitation, among them Laurel Hill in Philadelphia and Greenwood in Brooklyn. These rural cemeteries may well have helped create public interest in park scenery.

William Cullen Bryant, nature poet as well as editor of the *New York Evening Post*, was the first influential advocate of a large public park for New York City. Recognizing the need to set aside park land while open spaces still existed, he began publishing editorials on the subject in the *Evening Post* in the 1840s. Andrew Jackson Downing, distinguished Hudson River landscape gardener, took up the campaign in his magazine *The Horticulturist*. Both men had recently visited the royal parks of London and were enthusiastic about their popular use. And both also emphasized society's responsibility to the increasing population of immigrants, arriving in New York in larger numbers than ever as a result of the eruption of revolutions in Europe and of such catastrophes as the Irish potato famine.

In 1851, Mayor Ambrose C. Kingsland, newly elected with the support of the *Evening Post*, sent to the Common Council a message urging that the New York State legislature be petitioned for authority to acquire land for a public park. The legislature promptly responded by passing the First Park Act, authorizing the city of New York to purchase a beautiful wooded tract on the East River, stretching from Sixty-fourth Street to Seventy-fifth Street and west to Third Avenue. This area, known as Jones's Wood, was the one Bryant had first proposed for park use as early as 1844. But immediately opposition to this location developed on the grounds that the tract was too small. Even Bryant came to realize that it would not suffice for the expanding city. He, Downing, and others launched a campaign for another, much larger park, more centrally located on the Croton Reservoir in the middle of the island. The result of all this agitation was the passage, by the state legislature in 1853, of the Amended Park Act, authorizing the city of New York to acquire the central site, now Central Park, and at the same time to take Jones's Wood. Unfortunately, opposition to two parks was so powerful that, the following year, the Jones's Wood Act was repealed.

The next few years were spent in obtaining the land now comprising Central Park from 59th Street as far north as 106th Street;

the northward extension to 110th Street was not approved until 1859. From the beginning, partisan politics and lack of funds obstructed the development of the park. Finally, in 1857, the state legislature removed the park management from the Democratic mayor and the city government and entrusted it to a theoretically nonpartisan board of commissioners. One of the board's first decisions was to appoint a superintendent to supervise the labor force under the general direction of the chief engineer, Egbert L. Viele, and it was this position for which Olmsted, at the suggestion of the commissioner he met at the seaside inn, decided at once to apply.

Since he was already acquainted with many prominent men in New York City, he had no difficulty in finding sponsors like Washington Irving, Peter Cooper, William Cullen Bryant, Whitelaw Reid, August Belmont, and Asa Gray. In his petition, endorsed by almost two hundred signatures, he stressed his previous success in managing agricultural labor. He also mentioned having studied English and European public grounds and having paid special attention to the policing of parks and the economical deployment of labor in them. Despite the fact that the commissioners knew him better as a "literary" than as a "practical" man, he overcame the competition of John W. Audubon, son of the famous ornithologist, and of Joel B. Nott, whose father was president of Union College. He was appointed superintendent in September 1857 at a salary of $1,500 a year.

Olmsted's initiation into his new duties was hardly pleasant. After arriving neatly dressed for his first tour of the park, he was escorted through foul-smelling bogs and swamps, full of the overflow from pigpens, slaughterhouses, and bone-boiling works tended by local squatters living in shacks. He was initially an object of amusement to the gangs of workmen already employed, who had no way of knowing that this slight young man, as the new superintendent of the largest public works project in New York, would soon convert their reluctant work force into a model of efficiency. To add to his burdens, he was under continual pressure from politicians to give a job to every workman who presented himself, regardless of qualifications. The financial panic of 1857 had made Central Park

the only likely employer for thousands of jobless men who represented a threat to public order as they demonstrated with placards
reading "Bread or Blood."

Olmsted was able to hire a number of these men and somehow
to arouse their interest in ditching, draining swampy areas, remov-
ing stone, and tearing down squatters' shacks. He demonstrated a
notable gift for matching men to jobs. He was a strict taskmaster,
but his strong emphasis on discipline was matched by a calculated
trust in his subordinates. He organized his workmen into groups and
subgroups, both giving responsibility to foremen and then holding
them strictly accountable. The workmen were soon vying with one
another to do well and to please their new boss.

"Greensward"

In October 1857, while Olmsted was engaged in clearing the
land, the Central Park commissioners made a public announcement
that represents the real birth of landscape architecture as we know
it in the United States. They advertised in the New York papers
a contest for a park design, offering a prize of $2,000 for the best
entry. At first, Olmsted had no intention of entering the competition. It was Calvert Vaux, the young English architect who had
been Downing's partner and had taken over the landscape gardening practice after Downing drowned in 1852, who decided to enter
and invited Olmsted to collaborate on a design. Olmsted hesitated
out of consideration for Egbert Viele, the chief engineer who was
technically his superior and was himself entering the competition.
But when Viele showed contemptuous indifference as to whether
Olmsted should participate, Olmsted enthusiastically accepted
Vaux's proposal. Vaux had little idea at this time of Olmsted's
latent talent for landscape design. He was clearly impressed, however, by the fact that his prospective partner was developing an
intimate knowledge of the grounds and could provide accurate information about their topography beyond the information available
to competitors.

During the winter months, the two men worked together at night, or whenever Olmsted could get away from his supervisory duties, devising the best solutions they could for the numerous problems and restrictions of the dreary park site. The rules of the contest specified that each entry should embody certain features: four or more east-west crossings between 59th and 106th Streets; a parade ground of twenty to forty acres; three playgrounds of three to ten acres each; a site for a future exhibition or concert hall; a site for an ornamental fountain and one for a prospect tower; a flower garden of two to three acres and a design for it; and a place for a winter skating rink. The cost was to be limited to the one and a half million dollars allocated by the legislature.[2]

Olmsted and Vaux finished their plan under the signature "Greensward" and delivered it on the very last day of the competition, 1 April 1858. The commissioners invited Edward Kemp, who had worked with Joseph Paxton on Birkenhead Park, and a French engineer connected with the improvement to the Bois de Boulogne to advise them. The winners were announced on 28 April, Olmsted and Vaux taking first prize with Plan No. 33, the last of the thirty-three sets of drawings in the contest. Commending the winning design, the *New York Times* wrote: "There can be little doubt that in its essential features the plan of Messrs. Olmsted and Vaux embraces all the leading requisites of a great Park . . . adapted not only to the nature of the particular grounds in question, but to the prospective wants of our City also . . . we fortunately possess in Mr. Olmsted a Superintendent capable of carrying out our wishes, and honest enough to be safely entrusted with our interests."[3]

The brilliance of the plan that Olmsted and Vaux submitted is the result of their success in taking a narrow, largely barren rectangular plot in the middle of Manhattan and transforming it into a varied, yet coherent rural park. While the design was boldly original, it was firmly rooted in the traditions of English landscape art. Vaux was an Englishman by birth, and Olmsted had been greatly attracted to English scenery during his trips abroad. Central Park clearly reflects the developments in English park design during the eighteenth century, including the landscape gardening revolution led by such men as poet Alexander Pope and essayists Joseph Addison and Richard Steele. These men disliked the prevailing emphasis on the classical symmetry and formality of long avenues in royal gardens like Hampton Court during that era. Addison especially disliked the current fashion for topiary gardening, the practice of training trees and shrubs into odd or ornamental shapes. Landscape designers like Lancelot Brown (who came to be known as Capability Brown because of his propensity for seeing the "capabilities" in the places on which he worked) and Humphry Repton began to design in the new naturalistic style, producing striking compositions of pastoral scenery by using the gently curving line.

As the eighteenth century progressed, opposition developed to the school of Brown and Repton. Uvedale Price and Richard Payne Knight led the crusade against a school whose taste they considered insipid and dull because the sweeping drives and smoothly rounded hills it produced were too soft and tame. Real nature was, for Price and Knight, wilder and more exciting. They called for a gardening style they termed "picturesque." They were using the term in a new way, since they wanted to employ gnarled trees and rocky crags to create a rough, savagely dramatic, and melancholy effect.

The development of English landscape gardening in the eighteenth century provided important precedents for Olmsted and Vaux in creating Central Park, allowing them to work with spatial relationships in a new way and to make country scenery look as if man had had little hand in it at all. Their design actually represents a harmonizing of both sides of the argument that had raged during the preceding century. The carriage drives they planned were gently winding like those of Brown and Repton, whereas the forested Ramble, with its Rustic Arch, Cave, and Belvedere Castle, was ruggedly picturesque in the manner of Price and Knight. This harmony may, however, have been largely accidental since the two collaborators really had somewhat limited choices in planning Central Park. The terrain, with its poor soil, numerous outcroppings, and scrubby trees, must have influenced the form and style, and Olmsted and Vaux wisely capitalized on the easy, undulating outlines, on the one hand, and the rocky scenery, on the other.

They followed the lead of Humphry Repton in a striking technique for presenting their plan. Repton was famous for his "Red Books," which were proposed designs bound in beautiful red leather for his clients. In each book he would incorporate sketches of the existing landscape with ingenious hinged-flap overlays of exactly what he projected. Olmsted and Vaux used a similar "before and after" presentation, submitting pencil sketches or photographs of existing conditions in various locations of the park, juxtaposed with pencil or oil sketches of the same scenes as they envisioned them after the park was complete.

In the descriptive report they submitted with their "Greensward" plan, they explained that the site divided itself naturally into upper and lower sections. North of the old reservoirs, square receiving pools supplying the city with water from the Catskills, the land had bold and sweeping horizon lines representing the "highest ideal that can be aimed at for a park under any circumstances."[4] This area was to be left as wild as possible. The southern section, more heterogeneous, required a more varied treatment. Its most prominent feature was the rocky, wooded hillside immediately south of the reservoirs. The central and western portion was irregular tableland, while the eastern portion had graceful undulations adapted to grassy open vistas. At the extreme south end, some rugged ground and rocky bluffs stood out sharply from flat meadows.

Olmsted and Vaux took into account the constantly increasing population and commerce of New York City in a way no previous planners had done. They also realized that the very creation of Central Park would accelerate the occupation of the adjoining land. The position and length of the park on the narrow island were sure to make it, sooner or later, a serious obstacle to crosstown traffic. How could the four east-west transverse roads mandated by the rules of the competition be reconciled with the sense of north-south unity that had to be achieved throughout the park? The designers solved the problem by an unprecedented feat of futuristic engineering that constituted the most brilliant stroke of the "Greensward" plan. The four roads were sunk in deep-walled trenches hidden below the general surface of the park, keeping noisy business traffic from interfering in any way with the more leisurely pleasure traffic. Central Park thus contained the first example of the traffic underpass in the United States.

Likewise, Olmsted and Vaux also were ingenious in separating vertically even the different modes of pleasure traffic within the park. Pedestrian walks, bridle paths, and carriage drives were kept separate from one another and never crossed except at over- and underpasses in the form of cast-iron bridges or stone and brick archways. Nowhere were there any dangerous intersections.

In their design, the collaborators gave full expression to the democratic nature of the enterprise. Central Park was not conceived of as merely an ornamental pleasure ground for the upper classes. An early description noted that "the primary purpose of the park is to provide the best practicable means of healthful recreation for the inhabitants of all classes."[5] Rich and poor alike would find release in it from the monotony of the grid system of city streets and from the congestion of the urban environment. Olmsted and Vaux totally accepted the pastoral conventions that characterized rural scenery as an elevating place of peace and harmony removed from the distractions of the city. They gave full credence to the widely held belief of their age in the regenerative powers of nature in purging the ills of civilization. The park landscape was to be at least as important in its capacity to affect men's character as it was to delight their senses. Especially important, therefore, were to be the therapeutic effects of the scenery upon the working classes that could not afford to spend their leisure in the country or in travel.

Thus Olmsted and Vaux emphasized the predominantly rural character of Central Park, to which they subordinated both architectural and engineering features. They were unable to reduce its heterogeneous surface, largely formed of solid rock, to the simplicity of pastoral scenery. But they did succeed in treating the varieties of landscape so as to suggest to the imagination an unlimited range of rural conditions. The one chief exception to this policy was the area of the Mall and the adjoining Bethesda Fountain and Terrace. In a democratic park they felt that a grand promenade would be essential to encourage groups of citizens to congregate, and they

Central Park: For a competition held in 1857–58 to obtain a plan for what was to become Central Park, Olmsted and Vaux submitted the winning entry. Work on the park was still progressing in the summer of 1865 when this lithograph was made by John Bachmann and J. Bein. (Courtesy of the J. Clarence Davies Collection of the Museum of the City of New York)

incorporated this one tightly knit complex of formality into the southern section. The broad Mall, where large crowds were expected to gather, was a long straight axis flanked by a double column of elms and paved to accommodate the pounding of feet. The beautifully carved stone staircase descending to the circular terrace and fountain was an elegant climax to this important formal feature.

Architect in Chief for Central Park

Pleased with Olmsted's work as superintendent and his part with Vaux in winning the competition, the Board of Commissioners of Central Park made Olmsted architect in chief in May 1858 and raised his salary to $2,500 a year. The two designers were authorized to carry out their plan, and Olmsted was given the responsibility of employing and directing labor and of policing the park. By the autumn of 1858 over 2,500 laborers were at work, and an impressive amount of construction and planting had been done. By winter the public ice-skating for which the park soon became famous had begun. There had previously been few bodies of water within the city that were suitable for safe winter skating, but Central Park changed all that. Attendance records for the early years reveal that more visitors entered the park in January than in July, a fact that can only be explained by the popularity of skating. From the earliest winters in the park, artists like Winslow Homer captured the gaiety and robust movement of the scene, and Currier and Ives lithographs helped popularize the city's newest attraction.

While in later years Olmsted frequently expressed the feeling that credit for the park's artistic success belonged equally to Vaux and himself, he took individual credit for the organization and management of the work. Almost totally immersed in every operation, he realized that the finished design was to be achieved not on the drawing board but pragmatically on the grounds. He discovered early that, in planting, smaller trees were more likely to thrive than larger ones, so he had constantly to imagine the scale of the future when the trees would grow and fill in the outlines of the plan. He proved himself an accomplished social engineer in supervising the thousands of men working in subdivided crews on the various tasks of the huge project. No heavy machinery existed at that time to move the millions of cubic yards of stone, earth, and topsoil into or out of the park; the work had to be done solely by manpower and horsepower. George E. Waring, Jr., an expert in sanitary engineering, was responsible for draining and pond excavation, devising miles of drainage pipe underlying the new topsoil. W. H. Grant was the authority on road design. Ignaz A. Pilat, an Austrian who had studied in the Imperial Botanical Gardens in Vienna, became chief landscape gardener, in charge of two nurseries established within the park to cultivate seedling plants. Olmsted's colleagues and workmen developed a deep loyalty to their boss.

He cared as much for the daily life of the park, for making it a place where people might enjoy themselves, as for the designing of it. He planned for such amenities as rustic shelters, arbors, benches, a ladies' pavilion, and the pasturing of sheep and lambs for the amusement of children. He was concerned, too, about the park's maintenance in an orderly way, recognizing the need to educate the public in its proper use. Sensitive to criticism that the unenclosed park might easily fall victim to vandals, he took special pride in making visitors feel its distinctiveness without making them also feel unduly restricted. He obtained the right to have his own force of park keepers under his immediate supervision and to keep out regular city police. He carefully selected and trained these park keepers to protect the park but also to ensure the comfort and safety of all visitors. The *Times* reported approvingly, in November 1858, "The Police regulations are strictly enforced, and the whole work is so perfectly systematized that everything proceeds with the quiet regularity of a private establishment."[6]

From its beginning Central Park attracted widespread interest among New Yorkers, causing marked changes in the recreational habits of a large population that had never before been exposed to such a variety of pastimes. In addition to ice-skating in winter, boating and regularly scheduled band concerts developed a large following in summer. A fourteen-acre cricket and baseball ground was soon to be provided for participants in these sports. In all seasons, strollers on foot had miles of walks to explore in the lower park alone. Among the more affluent classes, both pleasure driving in carriages and horseback riding became fashionable after the opening of the winding park roads. Good pavements had not been available before, and relatively few carriages had been kept for pleasure driving. Still fewer horses had been kept for horseback riding in the city. Now, new tastes suddenly developed among all classes of citizens.

As the first real park designed in the United States, Central Park set a standard for landscaped park work that has not been materially improved in subsequent years. Olmsted and Vaux's "Greensward" plan represents the real beginning of the profession of landscape architecture in this country, though the term itself was not yet in use. The term then applied was "landscape gardening," a reference to those few practitioners like Andrew Jackson Downing who were mainly occupied with the adornment of property around country houses and public buildings. What Olmsted and Vaux did was to transform an elegant horticultural art to an exact scientific discipline involving the total arrangement and treatment of the landscape for human use and enrichment. And the achievement of Central Park was sufficient to elevate the two designers at a single step to a position of eminence.

By the summer of 1859, the work force on the park had grown to over 3,600 (the largest it was ever to be), partly as the result of public demand to push construction. In the fall, worn out by his heavy responsibilities, Olmsted was given a leave of absence by the park commissioners to undertake a six-weeks' study tour of English and European parks. Five hundred dollars was appropriated for his expenses. Although he needed a vacation from work, it was typical of him that he expended tremendous energy in seeing every park he could, constantly comparing conditions abroad with the accomplishments and possibilities of Central Park.

Olmsted revisited Birkenhead Park, this time obtaining full particulars of its construction, maintenance, and management. He then inspected parks in Birmingham and London. In Paris he met Adolphe Alphand, head of the Department of Roads and Bridges,

and spent two weeks visiting all the pleasure grounds and promenades in and around Paris, including the parks at Versailles, St.
Cloud, and the Bois de Vincennes. He made eight trips to study
the Bois de Boulogne before proceeding to Brussels, Lille, and
finally to Dublin and Cork in Ireland, where he sailed for home. He
was fully satisfied after his whirlwind travels that Central Park
rivaled, if it did not surpass, what was being done abroad.

As Olmsted once more became actively absorbed in the affairs of
the park, his relations with one of the commissioners, Andrew Haswell Green, became increasingly strained. Just before Olmsted left
for Europe, the Central Park Board had appointed Green their
comptroller. Previously the management of the park had been
largely in Olmsted's hands as architect in chief, and he had considerable freedom in his work. Upon his return, however, he discovered that Green was exercising absolute control over all park
expenditures and was usurping Olmsted's authority to carry out the
"Greensward" plan. At issue was the antagonism of two strong-
willed, often autocratic public servants, both equally devoted to the
park.

Green was a staunch advocate of Olmsted and Vaux's design and
was determined, as a conscientious administrator, to see it implemented strictly within the appropriations voted by the New York
State legislature. He was inclined to distrust the practical judgment
of Olmsted, whom he considered extravagant and only a novice in
park planning. Thus, as newly appointed comptroller, he resolved
to oversee personally every cent expended on the park's development. On the other side, Olmsted felt he had already proved himself in his work and, furthermore, had done the job economically.
He was resentful at not being given the leeway he felt a creative
artist must have. Overly sensitive in thinking that his reputation as
a man of honor and honesty was at stake, he worked himself up
to writing a letter of resignation to the park commissioners in January 1861. After promising him that he would regain control over
the park work and would not have to get the comptroller's approval
for every penny spent, the commissioners persuaded him to with-
draw his resignation.

During this same period, the commissioners, who were also in charge of laying out Manhattan north of 155th Street, demonstrated their general approval of Olmsted and Vaux's efforts on Central Park by appointing them landscape architects and designers for the new project. This was the first time the two men had the opportunity to make suggestions about the future growth of a large city area. Even Andrew Haswell Green was sufficiently pleased with their accomplishments to invite them to Worcester, Massachusetts, to help design the grounds of his family estate. In addition, they were asked to collaborate on designing grounds for the Hartford Retreat for the Insane.

Civil War Years

With the outbreak of the Civil War in April 1861, a move was immediately afoot to suspend further work on Central Park. Volunteers from hastily assembled regiments of the city drilled in the park. Olmsted himself organized a home guard of more than a hundred park keepers and drilled them on Sundays. He encouraged his men to enlist and offered his own resignation in preparation for undertaking some form of service to the Union. The commissioners once more refused to accept it, feeling that a continuation of work in the park was desirable to boost public morale and also that any interruption of work at this point would seriously jeopardize construction already under way. The pace of activity was modified, however, when Olmsted was granted a leave of absence at reduced salary to serve in Washington as executive secretary of the United States Sanitary Commission, newly established to supervise medical care of the Union forces. Calvert Vaux and Ignaz Pilat were left to go on with the park work, which continued throughout the war.

Although Olmsted became heavily involved for more than two years with the demanding work of the Sanitary Commission, he returned at intervals to New York and to Central Park. But Andrew Haswell Green's renewed interference in park affairs made life difficult for the designers. Vaux found himself even less able than Olmsted to work with Green, and relations finally reached the breaking point. Their letter of resignation in May 1863 was signed "Olmsted and Vaux, Landscape Architects." In accepting the resignation, the commissioners also used the designation "Messrs. Olmsted and Vaux, Landscape Architects," and placed on record the commissioners' "unabated confidence" in the partners' "high artistic taste and in their superior professional abilities."[7]

This exchange marks the first official use of the term "landscape architect," although a map of Central Park used in the annual park report issued in January 1863 contains the term, and the partners may have employed it privately before that date. At first, Vaux was more enthusiastic about the title than Olmsted, who was bothered by the "miserable nomenclature" and accepted it only for lack of a better one.[8] He gradually became accustomed to it, however, and used it frequently in his successive professional firms.

At the time of the partners' resignation from Central Park, Olmsted was so physically and mentally exhausted from his heavy organizational responsibilities for the Sanitary Commission that he thought seriously about leaving the Commission as well. He was undecided about continuing in the profession of landscape architecture. He considered joining Edwin L. Godkin in founding an independent weekly newspaper—a publication that did eventually take hold as *The Nation* after Olmsted had gone west. His financial situation was serious: he was unable to support his large family without relying upon his father. At this depressed point in his life, a new possibility for exercising his talents arose in the form of an unexpected call in 1863 to manage the Mariposa Estate, a large gold mining company in California. Since he had no clear prospects in the East, the large salary offered at Mariposa in addition to an idealistic desire to help civilize the Western frontier induced him to resign from the Sanitary Commission and to accept the call.

Although Olmsted's connection with the Mariposa Estate proved ultimately to be a mistake, he established himself more firmly as a landscape architect during his residence in the Far West. He produced preliminary plans for a campus, village, and park for the new College of California (now the University of California at Berkeley), a design for a new cemetery at Oakland, and preliminary

drawings—not carried out—for Golden Gate Park in San Francisco.
He also kept in touch with the progress of operations in Central
Park through Calvert Vaux but saw little likelihood of ever re-
establishing working arrangements with the commissioners. In 1865,
however, Vaux began writing frequently, urging Olmsted to return
to New York, not only because of Central Park but because Vaux
had been consulted by officials of the neighboring city of Brooklyn
about a possible large new park there.

It was Vaux who cleverly manipulated Andrew Haswell Green
into returning Central Park to the control of the landscape architects, and Vaux was also responsible for obtaining the park work in
Brooklyn. But he was reluctant to undertake these responsibilities
without the collaboration of Olmsted. Vaux had previously felt
"wholly incompetent," he argued, to design Central Park without
Olmsted's assistance, and now he felt he needed Olmsted again in
Brooklyn for the "translation of the republican art idea in its highest
form into the acres we want to control."[9] With the failure of the
Mariposa Estate, Olmsted was in a position to return east and
finally agreed to Vaux's requests to resume the partnership. In July
1865 they were reappointed landscape architects for Central Park,
at a salary of $5,000 a year.

Prospect Park

By November, Olmsted was back in New York, eager to resume
activities on Central Park as well as to embark on the Brooklyn park
work that would constitute the second crowning achievement of
Olmsted and Vaux. In Central Park his attention focused on the
upper portion extending from 106th to 110th Streets, added to the
park after the original land had been designated. Here a splendid
opportunity existed for picturesque treatment: a wealth of scattered
boulders in addition to a great deal of fixed rock provided unusual
possibilities for new paths and bridges and for distinctive artistry
in planting.

During this period Brooklyn was an independent municipality
separate from New York City, and the popularity of Central Park

aroused in the populace of Brooklyn a desire for a similar pleasure ground. Seven possible locations for a park had been chosen in 1860. Toward the end of the Civil War, while Olmsted was still in California, Vaux was called in for advice on a proposed site divided into two unequal pieces by Flatbush Avenue, a broad thoroughfare much used for public travel. Vaux objected to the inclusion of the avenue and recommended selling off the smaller portion northeast of it while at the same time doubling the area south and west.

On his return Olmsted concurred fully in Vaux's recommendations, and in January 1866 the partners submitted to the Board of Commissioners of Prospect Park a plan demonstrating that the division of the park site by Flatbush Avenue would seriously interfere with a sound design. By shifting the boundaries so as to keep the park entirely on the west side of the avenue, the commissioners would insure sufficient low ground for a large lake and for the extensive rural scenery necessary for the "sense of enlarged freedom" that is always "the most certain and the most valuable gratification afforded by a park."[10]

The plan was adopted, and in May, Olmsted and Vaux were formally appointed landscape architects and superintendents for Prospect Park, at a salary of $8,000 a year. Although field work was begun in July, not until 1868 did the New York State legislature complete, through addition of a crucial twelve-block area along the Ninth Avenue side, the acquisition of all the land included in the present park. As the work progressed, Olmsted became increasingly enthusiastic about it despite the difficulties of attempting to carry on operations in the northern section for over two years without final control over the Ninth Avenue stretch. One great advantage Olmsted and Vaux enjoyed in designing Prospect Park, in contrast to Central Park, was a minimum of political interference. The annual reports of the commissioners, under the enlightened guidance of their chairman James S. T. Stranahan, reveal the harmony and sympathetic understanding between them and the landscape architects. Even in the matter of boundaries, it was not the commissioners but the state legislature that slowed down operations.

When, at the end of 1873, the funds regularly appropriated for

Prospect Park came to an end, Olmsted and Vaux felt enormously pleased with their accomplishments. They were in the public eye in a way they had not been before. As had been the case with Central Park, Olmsted's part was larger than Vaux's in bringing the plan into physical shape on the site, and the details of the park were implemented largely under his personal direction. Just about all that remained to be done, whenever funds should become available, was the replacement of a few temporary wooden structures with permanent stone ones. In addition, the partners urged the completion of the main entrance on an oval plaza at the northern tip of the park. They advocated, for the park gateway, a handsome structure with an arcade, and they even designed and laid the pavement needed to carry out this feature. It took almost a quarter century, however, before the huge Soldiers' and Sailors' Arch was erected to commemorate the Union forces of the Civil War. The present monumental entranceway, designed by McKim, Mead, and White, was erected at the same time.

Prospect Park is no less a masterpiece than Central Park, and in some ways it can be considered more successful as a rural park. Certainly the rolling and well-wooded site of the Brooklyn park made the task of Olmsted and Vaux much easier than it had been on the rocky spine of Manhattan. They were able to adjust its boundaries to create a compact, well-rounded chunk of land in the shape of an arrowhead. Then, too, in Prospect Park there was no crosstown traffic to contend with and no such obstructions as the municipal reservoirs in Central Park. Planting was also far easier to do and to maintain in Prospect Park, where the soil was deeper and the areas possible to cultivate were more widespread. Finally, the designers were able to insist that cultural institutions planned for the future should not take up park land, as would happen with the Metropolitan Museum of Art in Central Park, but should be given separate territory outside the park proper.

The 1866 plan for Prospect Park combines the three types of landscapes that Olmsted and Vaux considered important for city dwellers to experience—an expansive, gently rolling meadow, a hilly woodland, and an extensive lake. As soon as one enters the park at

what is today called Grand Army Plaza, he is immediately transported far from the city environment by a continuous mound surrounding the park just inside its walls. This high ridge of earth,
thickly planted with trees and shrubs, is one of the most brilliant
innovations of the designers, providing an effective optical barrier
to the urban scene and an instant illusion of being in the country.
Immediately, one is confronted with an extended view of the 75-
acre Long Meadow that opens majestically before him. This is one
of the great open spaces of any city in the world, illustrating well
the psychological effect of curving space. Olmsted and Vaux knew
precisely what kind of pastoral effect they wanted: "The imagination of the visitor is thus led instinctively to form the idea that a
broad expanse is opening before him."[11] As one gazes, he is irre-
sistibly pulled toward the seemingly endless greensward, skirted by
groves of trees, where the Long Meadow curves first to the right
and then out of sight altogether.

Prospect Park provides a number of such spatial sequences ranged
on serially connected sight lines. Perhaps the most pronounced
sequence pulls one down the left side of the Long Meadow toward
a small pond that leads finally to the triple Nethermead Arches,
where four paths meet without interfering with one another: the
bridle path, the stream bed, the pedestrian walk, and the central
drive, which is carried over all the others. Eventually, regardless of
where one enters the park, all the walks and drives meet at the summit of Lookout Hill, the highest ground in the vicinity, providing
a spectacular view of the ocean and the whole outer harbor of New
York. Olmsted and Vaux planned three special areas where visitors
were to congregate: the Lookout Concourses on Lookout Hill; the
Concert Grove at the northeast end of the lake; and a terrace restaurant midway between the two. Unfortunately, the first now
stands abandoned and overgrown, the second has had its view of the
lake obliterated, and the third was never built.

As Olmsted worked on Prospect Park, he came more and more
to look upon his efforts as part of the historical development of
cities. His annual report to the commissioners in 1868 included a
history of street systems from the Middle Ages onward. As might

have been expected from his earlier writings on the South, he based his approach to urban history on a democratic concern for all classes of citizens, emphasizing the importance of equal access to the park for all residents of Brooklyn. The 1866 plan for Prospect Park had already demonstrated the comprehensiveness of the vision the partners had for the New York of the future: "We regard Brooklyn as an integral part of what today is the metropolis of the nation, and in the future will be the centre of exchanges for the world, and the park in Brooklyn, as part of a system of grounds, of which the Central Park is a single feature, designed for the recreation of the whole people of the metropolis and their customers and guests from all parts of the world for centuries to come."[12]

Olmsted and Vaux envisioned a system of linear green spaces extending throughout and linking the two cities. Although this great connected park system never became a full reality, they did succeed in designing two wide boulevards or parkways in Brooklyn based on the plan of the Avenue de l'Impératrice (now Foch) in Paris. Both Ocean Parkway, linking Prospect Park and the Coney Island beaches on the Atlantic, and Eastern Parkway, constructed as a handsome approach to the park from the east, featured central pleasure drives for carriages, flanked on either side by pedestrian paths that were, in turn, bordered by service roads for delivery and local traffic with sidewalks along their outside edges. Roads and pathways were separated from one another by strips of turf and rows of trees.

Increased Political Interference

Meanwhile, the association of Olmsted and Vaux with Central Park continued to be marked by political interference. This time they watched the creeping power of the group headed by Boss William Marcy Tweed and the eventual control of the park by that group as the passage of a new city charter was manipulated through the state legislature. Until 1870, the commissioners of Central Park had been appointed at state level and ruled by the inflexibly honest, if imperious and sometimes petty, Andrew Haswell Green. Now the infamous Tweed Ring took over the park under the guise of the newly created New York City Department of Public Parks, and Olmsted and Vaux, totally disregarded, were forced to resign in protest against the chicanery. For nearly a year they had to watch the arrogant misuse of their creation by Tweed and his cronies. In places where low growth and picturesque obscurity had been carefully achieved, the new management destructively pruned the shrubs, smoothed the surface, and trimmed the trees of branches to a height of ten to fifteen feet from the ground. Green, who remained loyal to the original plan, was a helpless minority of one on the new Central Park Board. All that Olmsted and Vaux could do was try to appeal to the public through the press.

After the exposure and collapse of the Tweed Ring in 1871, the partners were once more reappointed landscape architects for Central Park, and they were instrumental in having Frederic E. Church, the distinguished landscape painter, added to the Board of Commissioners: "We were anxious . . . that the art element [of Central Park] should be recognized—that the public utility of devotion to art and the study of Nature in a public service of this kind should be recognized."[13] Even under these circumstances, however, harsh realities had to be faced. The Tweed Ring's graft had left the Parks Department badly in debt. Then, the indiscriminate thinning out of plant material was aggravated by the severe winter of 1871–72, which killed almost eight thousand trees. Olmsted had also to repair the physical destruction done by the Ring to the Central Park meadows. And he found that the park keepers, demoralized under the Tweed regime, now included many men physically unfit and indifferent to their responsibilities. He obtained permission to reorganize the park keepers' force, but in disturbing the recently introduced system of patronage, he incurred a storm of political protest.

In 1872 Olmsted and Vaux decided, for mutual convenience, to dissolve their partnership. They had frequently argued in the past. Among other reasons, Vaux was resentful that too much credit for the designing of Central Park was regularly assigned to Olmsted and too little to himself. Olmsted had tried to correct this impression, but Vaux was extraordinarily sensitive on this point. Although the partnership for private business came to an end, they continued to work together on the New York parks and on other projects from time to time. Olmsted remained landscape architect for Central Park, with duties of superintendence, while Vaux became consulting landscape architect.

But Olmsted's position in the park was becoming increasingly precarious. The next crisis erupted in 1873, when a change in the bylaws of the Park Board threatened to remove control of the park keepers from him and give it over to the regular city police. The trouble was patched up but was indicative of things to come. Until the end of 1877, he did what he could to maintain the park but was severely handicapped by inadequate appropriations and a corrupt patronage system dominated by Tammany politicians. He recognized, for example, the need to repair the park drainage system, one of the most extensive pieces of work installed anywhere in the country, comprising ninety-five miles of buried pipe and tile. No action was taken at this time.

During these last years of service to Central Park, Olmsted was also engaged in laying out Morningside and Riverside parks on the upper west side of Manhattan. He recognized the importance of both of these parks as part of an extended chain of green spaces connected to Central Park at its northern end, yet he had also begun to see the need for other types of public facilities such as athletic fields and grounds for fairs and great public ceremonies. Nevertheless, while finding the "practical public uses" for Morningside Park "unusually limited," he succeeded in solving the park's technical problems in his 1873 design.[14] But he was much happier with his plan for Riverside Park in 1875. Because of the steep grades and frequent undulations of the site, he developed a design combining an avenue, called Riverside Drive, with the park itself. The highlights were a terraced carriage drive, three miles long, overlooking the Hudson River and a handsome foot promenade commanding the same view.

More Designs for New York City

In 1874 New York City, until then limited to Manhattan Island, annexed the western portion of Westchester County, which later became part of the Bronx. This annexation, designated as the twenty-third and twenty-fourth wards, was the first official step toward consolidation of what would become the Greater City of New York. Olmsted was asked to design a street system and plan for a rapid-transit steam railway to serve the new wards, located north of Manhattan. His collaborator this time was not Calvert Vaux but John James R. Croes, a civil and topographical engineer who had worked for the Croton Water Board.

Their reports, presented in 1876 and 1877, seem to have been written largely by Olmsted. They advocated departing from the monotonous grid or rectangular block system that had been followed in the division of property in New York City since the early part of the nineteenth century. Under this system houses had been squeezed onto narrow lots, with most natural contours lost. The grid plan had tended to foster poorly ventilated housing without any alleys for the removal of ashes and garbage.

Olmsted had attempted to break away from the grid system when he designed a preliminary street plan for the hilly Riverside section on the upper west side of Manhattan, but the Board of Commissioners had rejected the innovation as inappropriate for a commercial city. Thus the Riverside section was finally laid out, at considerable expense, on a modified grid. Now, once again, Olmsted urged the commissioners to reject the grid system in order to provide maximum social benefits in keeping with the natural topography of the annexed area.

The design that Olmsted and Croes settled on for the two new wards was a striking combination of railroad engineering and picturesque park planning. They first determined the site of a loop of tracks that would encircle the area and a connecting line that would cut through the middle. The proposed rapid-transit line had to be as straight and level as possible and also had to afford direct transportation between all desired points. Much of the ingenuity of the plan lay in the principle of grade separation that Olmsted had first used in Central Park. Nowhere would the railway line cross streets at the same level, and it would interfere only minimally with property divisions. It would be far cheaper to build, less ugly, and much quieter than the new elevated railways then being built over the streets of Manhattan.

Having fixed the site of the railway line and main roads, Olmsted and Croes then devised a winding secondary road system for the residential sections, following closely the contours of the charming, hilly topography. Such a design, they argued, would actually be less expensive as well as more appropriate for a suburban district than a system of parallel streets. These interlocking roads would, like the primary thoroughfares, cross the railway line only at over- or underpasses. The designers felt that this area, combining the conveniences of the city with the healthfulness of the country, would be ideal for those New Yorkers who could afford suburban residences. It would have an attractiveness "far excelling in its kind that of any other locality in America,"[15] drawing and holding within the city limits people of means who would otherwise seek homes farther away. These detailed reports thus reflect Olmsted's continuing interest in conserving both land values and human values. For him, good planning and good living were inextricably tied together.

Unfortunately, before the remarkable proposal drawn up by Olmsted and Croes could be acted upon, the reform politicians who had broken the hold of the Tweed Ring were themselves thrown out of office by a reconstituted Tammany Hall group of Democrats who found a way to regain power under the new city charter. Olmsted's health broke down under systematic harassment by these Tammany politicians, who wanted to oust him from his job. At one point, he was forced to sue the city to collect his salary for several months in 1876. During 1877, articles critical of him appeared in various Tammany publications, arguing that Central Park was essentially finished and therefore required no further creative guidance from a salaried landscape architect. The interests of these Tammany men were directed not toward the real needs of Central Park but toward the system served by the jobs that the park created.

Andrew Green, who had antagonized Olmsted and yet frequently fought on his side, lost his position in 1876. Once Green was gone, the park was more vulnerable than ever. Two years later, just after Olmsted requested and received a leave of absence on his doctor's orders, the Office of Design and Superintendence that he headed was summarily abolished. Even though he was still to be retained as consulting landscape architect, to be paid for his services as they might on occasion be requested, he realized that he had in effect been drummed out altogether. His friends immediately launched a campaign to have his dismissal rescinded. Obtaining the signatures of 185 prominent citizens of various callings, they addressed a forceful petition to the Board of Commissioners, but the Board simply restated adamantly its previous decision.

The fate of the proposal for the annexed twenty-third and twenty-fourth wards was not yet sealed when Olmsted left New York on an extensive European tour. Croes remained to defend the plans but was unsuccessful in persuading the politicians and real estate speculators to adopt them. Thus the opportunity to create a distinctive suburban district with an inexpensive and efficient rapid-transit system was lost.

"The Spoils of the Park"

Upon his return from Europe, Olmsted began to think seriously of leaving New York. His ties to the city had been gradually loosening for some time as his practice of landscape architecture expanded. Many of his clients were situated around Boston, and he had already started work on the Boston parks. After several summers in Cambridge and Brookline, he was ready for a permanent move to Massachusetts. Yet, even as he was abandoning New York, he still could not forget Central Park. Toward the end of 1881, he wrote a long pamphlet, "The Spoils of the Park," in which he defended his ideals for the park and explained the reasons for his failure to accomplish all he had wanted to do.

The subtitle of the work is: "With a Few Leaves from the Deep-laden Notebooks of 'A Wholly Unpractical Man.'" The tone is frequently ironic, sometimes bitterly so, as Olmsted plays upon the contrast between the words "practical" (in a narrow political sense) and "unpractical" (in the sense in which he was frequently regarded by his political opponents and a segment of the public). He makes the point that, far from being "unpractical" in his designs and in his management of the park, he has proved himself an expert. Privately printed in 1882, the pamphlet reflects his frustration after having struggled for more than two decades against political harassment in the operations of Central Park. "I fear that its ruin is inevitable," he wrote his friend Charles Loring Brace, "and it is very depressing to me."[16]

"The Spoils of the Park" reveals Olmsted's somewhat élitist attitude toward Central Park, an attitude that kept coming into conflict with the ever more insistent impulses of urban democracy during the Gilded Age. From the first, he had defined the park primarily as a work of art, with all its elements uniting in a single organic design. He continued to think of its chief benefits as visual and psychic, offering therapeutic escape from the expanding street grid of the commercial city. But while he felt that Central Park would offer release for all urban classes, he had provided mainly a highly contemplative kind of recreation that appealed to him personally and to members of his own cosmopolitan class. He was paternalistic in insisting that the rural scenery of the park would have a calming influence on the uncultivated working people of New York. And he was somewhat naive in believing that the natural simplicity of the pastoral landscape would promote communal feelings among all urban classes and minimize resentments over differences in wealth and fashion.

Hardly a year passed by since Olmsted and Vaux began working on Central Park that more prosaic, less enlightened minds than the designers' did not propose new projects to fill the "empty spaces." The park was not only a magnificent work of art but a municipal public works project. While Olmsted set his goals well into the future, feeling that the appearance of a "finished" landscape would require decades to be achieved, politicians frequently saw the park in short-range terms as vacant land to be filled with jobs and structures on a set schedule. Olmsted and Vaux only gradually came to recognize the dangers that structures in the park represented, for they were initially eager to promote educational enterprises. Thus they did not at first object to the siting of the Metropolitan Museum of Art within the park, but soon realized their error when the museum began expanding in all directions. They were eventually faced with the continual threat of new statues and monuments and proposed projects such as trotting speedways, world's fairs, churches, and circuses.

One objection to the rural landscape design of Central Park was that, with the erection of tall buildings surrounding it, its visible frame had become somewhat unrural and therefore the park should be given a more urban, architectural treatment. Already, since Olmsted's dismissal, vistas had been opened to allow Fifth Avenue, which he had carefully screened out with plantings, to be clearly visible from within. His argument, however, continued to be that, for most city residents, one of the most refreshing qualities of a park is that combination of spaciousness and mysterious intricacy associated with the distant open countryside, even where there can be no possibility of the most momentary illusion of actually being in the country.

Olmsted's pamphlet concluded with recommendations for remedial action. He advocated placing park management above politics, subject to review by "an unpaid board of citizens, so large, and of such established reputation . . . that there could be some rational confidence that they would exercise conservative control."[17] Unfortunately "The Spoils of the Park" is frequently obscure and difficult to read. Partly because of Olmsted's desire to protect some well-intentioned commissioners, it tends to be too general and to allude to people and events without sufficient clarification. Perhaps in part for this reason, it did not evoke the kind of editorial comment in the press that he expected. Many readers, in fact, misunderstood his main points and took the pamphlet as a tract for the civil-service reform so much in vogue in the 1880s. The most gratifying reaction came from a young reform-minded legislator, Theodore Roosevelt, then just starting his political career in Albany. Roosevelt responded immediately that he had read "Spoils" with great interest and could match every statement with corresponding experiences of his own. He volunteered to sponsor a bill in the state legislature incorporating Olmsted's proposals and suggested a list of distinguished citizens, including Olmsted, Vaux, and Frederic Church, to constitute a new Park Board. Nothing came of Roosevelt's plan, however.

After Olmsted moved his practice to Brookline, in the suburbs of Boston, he also became distressed at the changing fortunes of Prospect Park. His professional association with this park had been unusually harmonious because of the leadership of James S. T. Stranahan on the Brooklyn Park Commission. Olmsted still managed to visit the park about once a year and, during Stranahan's administration, considered such sections as the East Woods, Dairy District, and Nethermead especially charming. In 1882, however, a new city administration planned to replace Stranahan, who thereupon asked Olmsted's help in retaining his job. But after twenty-two years of dedicated service, Stranahan was removed, and by the mid-1880s the park was beginning to experience the same fate as Central Park.

Although Olmsted often claimed during this period that he had cut himself off from New York City and its affairs, he still had many friends and advocates there. In 1886, with Riverside and Morningside parks still unfinished, he was requested to examine their condition and complete construction. He agreed to work with Vaux provided they could be free from political pressures. In his final plan for Morningside Park, he reminded the commissioners that, because of their delay in acting upon his original proposal, it was no longer possible to create the interrelated park system connecting Morningside to Central Park that he had originally envisioned. Then, immediately after completing the project one year later, he resigned his position.

He had been urged to take up management of all the New York City parks again along with Vaux and considered the offer seriously for a time. "I don't want to have to come back to New York," he wrote to Vaux, "but I am not sure that I should not even do that rather than lose all chance of bringing the parks back to original principles so far as that is now possible. . . . There is nothing else that I care so much for."[18] Ultimately, however, facing squarely the political realities of New York, he rejected the offer. He was content to become an occasional consultant to the New York park commissioners.

Very near the end of his career, upon visiting Prospect Park in 1894, he learned that the Brooklyn park commissioners wanted to engage him again as consulting landscape architect. He made arrangements to have his firm visit the park twelve times a year. Recognizing that the work would probably be difficult and would involve further political disputes, he nevertheless felt it his professional duty to have his firm take on the job and see what it could do to get park operations returned as much as possible to his original concept. He knew, however, that the natural, rural style of design that he and Vaux had established in Prospect Park was no longer in fashion. Stanford White had recently been employed as an architect and was determined to transform the park, as far as possible, into something conspicuously classical and monumental. Olmsted speculated that White would attempt to make the park an "incongruous hybrid"[19] between the original unobtrusive design and a design of architectural beauty in the manner of Versailles. In his conjecture, Olmsted proved ultimately to be correct. The naturalistic style of architecture had indeed given way to the classical style, culminating in the Columbian Exposition of 1893, for which Olmsted himself had already designed the grounds.

Chapter Four

Other Parks and Planned Communities

Landscape Designs for San Francisco

Even while still working on Central Park, Olmsted and Vaux began to be employed by private institutions and individuals to give advice and to plan a variety of projects. The Hartford Retreat for the Insane and the Bloomingdale Asylum north of New York City asked them to design the grounds of these institutions. They were also called on for work on the grounds of the New Rochelle residence of shipowner E. K. Collins and of the country place of journalist Parke Godwin at Roslyn, Long Island. This sort of private work was interrupted, however, by the Civil War, and Olmsted did not pick it up again until he was in California managing the Mariposa Estate.

In 1864, while waiting in San Francisco for his family to arrive from the East, Olmsted was consulted on the new Mountain View Cemetery at Oakland, California. Here he was doing independent landscape architecture for the first time and had a free hand to design exactly what he thought was best. His plan proved to be a bold departure from what he had done in Central Park and shows that Olmsted was not dominated by preconceived notions or predilections but approached each job as a fresh challenge. He recognized that the English picturesque style of landscape would not be suitable to a semiarid climate. Instead, he chose a design of formal simplicity resembling a Mediterranean villa garden, using native plant materials, including oaks and cedars, that would not require extensive watering during the dry season. The broad central avenue of the cemetery had trees regularly spaced on either side. At the farthest end he placed a formal, terraced circle and fountain. Finally, the steep natural amphitheatre looking down toward the bay was enclosed with hedges and walls to protect it from the robust Pacific winds.

Olmsted became fascinated with the city of San Francisco. He foresaw that this raw western community would someday become internationally important and would slough off its association with the gold rush in California. In August 1865, the *San Francisco Bulletin* printed a long letter by Olmsted urging San Franciscans to undertake a great rural park on the order of Central Park. His suggestions so impressed the board of supervisors of the city that they engaged him, after his return to New York, to draft a park plan. Using maps and photographs, as well as a rough sketch he had made before leaving San Francisco, he did a thorough report that is an important pioneering work in city planning even though it was never officially adopted. He recognized, as he had with Central Park, the importance of planning for the future and argued the economic advantage of a design that would include from the beginning all the features that would likely ever be wanted.

As was customary with Olmsted, he was equally concerned with the commercial, social, and moral implications of his plan. Using the techniques of a modern public relations expert, he exhorted San Franciscans to accept the opportunity that a "liberally devised public pleasure ground with its accessories"[1] would offer the city in competing with New York, London, and Paris. But he also argued, on social and moral grounds, that a park would be a stabilizing influence on the restless and often transient population and would enable "all citizens to pursue commerce less constantly, to acquire habits of living healthily and happily from day to day."[2]

Acknowledging that San Francisco did not possess the soil or shade trees necessary for the landscape style of eastern or English parks, Olmsted pointed to the beauty of its small gardens. This feature led him to urge that ornamental parts of the park should be compact, protected from the direct action of the wind, and rich in detail. These parts should be integrated with an extensive system of walks, drives, and resting places that could be regulated without expensive police protection. The neighborhood should be of such a character as to invite the erection of high quality private houses and public buildings. Finally, the park should be so structured as to provide a firebreak separating and protecting the various districts of the expanding city in case fire ever broke out.

Olmsted's specific design for the park reveals how brilliantly he could find solutions to landscape problems using the materials at hand. For the promenade grounds within the park he proposed digging an excavation at least twenty feet deep, with the sides sloping down so as to have a nearly level bottom. Within the excavation he planned for riding trails and carriage drives as well as for broad walks. The lower parts of the banks would be turfed, and the slopes would be planted with shrubs and trees, with a thicket of hardy evergreens all along the top. Bridges would carry the city streets across the sunken promenade grounds at convenient intervals, and hydrants would be supplied to keep the dust down and to water the turf.

Although Olmsted was paid for his comprehensive and ingenious plan, the project was stalled at this point because necessary legislation could not be passed. Not until 1871 did San Francisco at last undertake what became Golden Gate Park. Then the city selected a different site and a new designer, William Hammond Hall, who immediately wrote to Olmsted for advice. The two men kept in touch periodically over the years. In the light of Olmsted's provision in his plan for a firebreak as part of the promenade grounds, it is ironic that, after the disastrous fire following the great earthquake of 1906, the closely built city blocks along the line that Olmsted had designated for the promenade were dynamited in a last desperate measure to keep the fire from spreading.

Olmsted's Work Expands

With the Civil War ended and with many American cities entering upon a period of dramatic growth, the achievement of Central

Park attracted the interest of city officials and civic leaders across the country who began to entertain the idea of developing their own rural parks. A wide variety of motives inspired these citizens. Fairmont Park in Philadelphia, for example, was considered an important source of protection for the city's water supply. A strong economic argument was frequently made for the construction of parks: after all, the building of Central Park had resulted in a spectacular increase in the value of the surrounding land. Still another factor was a strong moral imperative, an enlightened concern for the public well-being, that spurred on the efforts of many city fathers who believed that creating a rural park was not only a sound financial investment but a civic duty.

Something of the belief in progress that characterized the era can be seen in the formation, in 1865, of the American Social Science Association, of which Olmsted early became an officer. This organization was devoted, among other interests, to "the Advancement of Education, the Prevention and Repression of Crime, and the furtherance of Public Morality."[3] One of the most basic statements of Olmsted's position toward the rural parks movement appears in his preliminary report on the laying out of Prospect Park in Brooklyn in 1866:

The great advantage which a town finds in a park, lies in the addition to the health, strength, and morality which comes from it to its people. . . . The reason is obvious: all wealth is the result of labor, and every man's individual wealth is, on the whole, increased by the labor of every other in the community. . . . but as there cannot be the slightest exercise of skill of any kind, without the expenditure of force, it follows that, without recuperation and recreation of force, the power of each individual to labor wisely and honestly is soon lost.[4]

For Olmsted, good health and morality went hand in hand and were central concerns in his landscape designs. In keeping with the idealism of the age, beauty and appropriateness in architectural form were always related in his mind to moral objectives.

Hartford, Connecticut, began developing Bushnell Park not long after New York started Central Park, and in 1866 Baltimore opened

Druid Hill Park. That same year, Lieutenant Governor William Bross of Illinois, after looking at Olmsted's park plan for San Francisco, inquired whether the designer could do a park for Chicago. General Montgomery Meigs wrote to Olmsted, whom he had known during his days in the Sanitary Commission, about a park for Washington, D.C. William Dorsheimer, a prominent attorney in Buffalo, asked Olmsted and Vaux about the possibilities for a park there. Olmsted moved back also into the design of residential areas when his friend Howard Potter asked him to plan a cottage suburb at Long Branch, New Jersey. In 1867, Olmsted and Vaux were consulted for the first time about Philadelphia's Fairmont Park and also prepared reports for new parks in New Britain, Connecticut, and Newark, New Jersey. The next year they sent recommendations for a park in Albany, and in 1869 they were asked to lay out a maritime park in Providence, Rhode Island. The reputation of the Olmsted and Vaux firm was clearly expanding greatly in these years.

The advice given and recommendations submitted did not always lead to further work for the partners, and in some cases considerable time elapsed before any further business developed. Yet Olmsted was a realist, understanding that he could never expect all of his proposals to be accepted and implemented. What was most important to him was the growing national interest in parks and in the field of landscape architecture. The main business of the partners continued to be the New York City parks, but they welcomed additional work provided it allowed them to employ the same high standards they had developed. They soon devised a standard procedure that they felt was in keeping with a profession they wanted to make equal to such professions as medicine and law.

One of the partners, frequently Olmsted, would make a preliminary study of the grounds of a proposed work and consult with the client first of all about the general objectives the plan should achieve rather than about any specific design. For this advice they charged a moderate, never exorbitant, fee tempered to the client's pocketbook. They furnished each client a rate sheet: $100 to $200 for a preliminary survey plus traveling expenses; $2,000 to $5,000 for a large design. If their ideas were accepted and they agreed to do the job, the initial fee went on account. If, after preliminary consideration, they found that they could not in good conscience do the work, they withdrew.[5]

Olmsted and Vaux ordinarily declined to carry out any landscape design for which they did not have comprehensive responsibility. They took pains to dispel the prevalent notion that landscape architects were merely glorified nurserymen or gardeners employed to decorate grounds already graded and developed. Part of their responsibility, they realized, was to educate their clients, and through them the public in general, to regard landscape architecture as a new and distinctive profession that incorporated the skills of horticulture, architecture, and engineering. And, in keeping with the dignity of their profession, they made it a practice not to accept payments or favors from contractors whom they engaged on behalf of a client; they accepted payment only from the client himself. Nor did they go in for land speculation in an age which it would have been easy for them to do so, though they did occasionally accept a few lots as part of their payment.

Riverside, Tarrytown Heights, and Staten Island

The work that Olmsted and Vaux were doing in New York and other cities made them feel that "the most prominent characteristic of the present period of civilization has been the strong tendency of people to flock together in great towns."[6] Yet, by the late 1860s, Olmsted saw signs of another trend toward the formation of suburbs beginning to affect the more affluent classes. In 1868, the partners were invited by Emery E. Childs, of Chicago, to advise his newly formed Riverside Improvement Company. The project was a real-estate venture to establish a self-contained suburban village on 1,600 acres of land on the banks of the Des Plaines River, nine miles west of the center of Chicago.

Riverside was to become the earliest significant example in the United States of the use of landscape architecture in a real-estate subdivision project. The suburb remains today a monument to the enduring power of Olmsted and Vaux's extraordinary design, despite the fact that it has become surrounded by other less distinguished suburbs in the century since its beginnings. On his first visit to the site, Olmsted noted the advantages of the location. While the greater part of the land around Chicago was "low, flat, miry, and forlorn,"[7] the region bordering the Des Plaines River offered a promising contrast with its winding river banks covered with groves of trees.

Riverside proved to be a felicitous combination of rural scenery and civilized comfort. One of its major achievements was its inventive system of roads. Olmsted and Vaux provided for frostproof, rainproof roads and walks and thorough underground drainage. The curvilinear street plan, taking advantage of the natural features of the land, reflects the partners' consummate understanding of the way form affects the character of environment: the "gracefully curved lines, generous spaces, and the absence of sharp corners" of the streets were to suggest "leisure, contemplativeness, and happy tranquility."[8] The rural effect was heightened by the careful avoidance of curbs and by the placement of the roads in slight depressions so as to become almost invisible except when directly ahead of the rider or pedestrian.

According to the design, houses in Riverside were to be built at least a specified minimum distance from the roads and to be approached by private drives. Each individual homeowner would have to plant one or two trees between his house and the roadway. Houses were to be placed farther apart than was customary in cities, providing considerable privacy for indoor and outdoor domestic life. Yet they were not to be as far apart as large country estates but in visible communication and harmonious association with one another. Rather than placing shade trees at regular intervals along the streets as was often the custom, Olmsted and Vaux planted maples, elms, and horse chestnuts irregularly in order to provide foliage along the winding streets in great and varied masses.

At key points throughout the suburb, open spaces were to contribute a sense of sylvan beauty and calm as well as opportunities for recreation on common ground. Olmsted and Vaux saw to it, in fact, that some of the best land would be appropriated for unfenced public grounds in the manner of informal village greens, with play areas including croquet grounds and ball fields. The height of the milldam was to be raised to make the river wider for boating and skating, and a public drive and walk were to be constructed along the bank, along with boat landings, terraces, and rustic, vine-draped pavilions.

Although Riverside already contained the first out-of-town railway station on the main line leading out of Chicago, the partners recommended construction of a wide, tree-lined, six-mile parkway, with separated carriage roads, bridle paths, and walks, to connect the suburb with the outskirts of the city. Businessmen could thus combine recreation with the journey to work in Chicago by riding in a carriage or on horseback. And on holidays, people from the city could use the parkway to come for "rural fêtes" in Riverside.

The parkway was never built. Childs defaulted on his payments to the landscape architects before parkway construction was begun and, moreover, attempted to compromise their plan by building on the beautiful central open space, called the Long Common, which was the keystone of the whole design. Childs was restrained from doing so, but by 1870 the project was so disorganized that it was losing business for Olmsted and Vaux, and the partners resigned. Finally, the Chicago fire of 1871 and ensuing financial depression dimmed prospects further for Riverside by temporarily halting the sale of suburban real estate.

Yet Riverside survived and eventually flourished, partly because the careful plans that Olmsted and Vaux had originally drawn up were substantially followed. The unprecedented curving road system, with a controlled sweep of its own, was fortunately laid out early and provided a continuity that sustained the gradual growth of the suburb. Thus the designers were able to demonstrate that they could do for the suburb what they had done for the large city with Central and Prospect parks: break away from the uniformity of right angles and straight lines. As they had predicted, Riverside was successful in blending urban conveniences with the informal, picturesque charms of rural life. It is still largely unchanged in character today, is loyally defended by its residents, and has recently been declared a National Historic Landmark.

In the early 1870s, Olmsted and Vaux were engaged to lay out another suburban community at Tarrytown Heights, New York, a 900-acre tract of land twenty-five miles north of New York City in the region made famous by Washington Irving. The partners laid out the tract in 159 villa sites, but because of the irregular boundaries of the community, this design lacks the unity of Riverside. Some twenty years later, near the end of his career, Olmsted was asked by the Roland Park Company of Baltimore, Maryland, to serve as landscape architect for a development then four miles north of the Baltimore city line. During the intervening period Olmsted and his firm had been involved in many land subdivisions for private investors, but none was as important as Roland Park, which eventually came within the corporate limits of Baltimore. Although Roland Park lacks the overall unity of Riverside, it represents a striking use of topography in its employment of the cul-de-sac road along ridges and ravines. For this development, Olmsted also helped devise a set of deed restrictions governing the use of property and its maintenance in the operation of a community organization. This pioneering effort was imitated by later land developers.

During the same period as Riverside and Tarrytown Heights, Olmsted became involved in an attempt to make Staten Island, as yet sparsely settled, a more attractive and desirable suburb of New York City. From having lived there, he knew the island intimately and welcomed the opportunity to develop a community within easy reach of the city center. Thus far the island had been plagued with problems, including poor transportation on ferries and main roads, slow communication, and a reputation for breeding malaria. In July 1870, the *New York World* published an open letter by Olmsted that suggested organizing a commission for the improvement of the island. As a result, Olmsted, Henry Hobson Richardson, and Dr. Elisha Harris were appointed members of a committee of experts to draw up recommendations for an overall plan. Richardson, who was then a young architect, was at this time a neighbor of Olmsted on

Staten Island. Harris was one of the foremost public health physicians in the United States. The chairmanship of the commission was entrusted to Olmsted.

Their thorough report, integrating the skills and knowledge of public health doctors, geologists, and sanitary engineers with Olmsted's aesthetic and social theories, was a remarkable example of what nineteenth-century cooperative planning could produce. It offered a comprehensive fourteen-point plan, at an estimated cost of two to four million dollars, for improved ferry service to New York, better roads, attractive parks, and thorough drainage of low areas on the island. Though the connection between mosquitoes and malaria was not yet known, drainage was a sound approach to better health conditions. The report stressed the improved sanitation that could be achieved by uniting the various neighborhoods into one large community.

Unfortunately, because of the cost of the plan and also because the individual villages were unable to act together, the report was never adopted. Staten Island was destined to develop haphazardly, demonstrating the difficulty of attempting to change the character of an established community as opposed to planning a village like Riverside from the ground up.

Parks for Chicago

In the late 1860s and through the 1870s, the Olmsted firm (the partnership of Olmsted and Vaux lasted only until 1872) began a series of major projects—notably the Chicago, Buffalo, Montreal, and Boston parks—that made it even more prominent throughout the country. In addition to planning Riverside, Olmsted persuaded the city fathers of Chicago to allow his firm to design their new South Park. The site of this proposed park was hardly ideal. The Lower Division, later to become Jackson Park, consisted of swampy sand dunes fronting on Lake Michigan, and the Upper Division, subsequently Washington Park, was flat, relatively treeless prairie. While the dull prairie was entirely different from the rocky formations Olmsted and Vaux had had to contend with in Central Park, they realized that a flat site was not necessarily undesirable in a public park: "It should especially be considered that where there is a broad meadow with ever so little obvious play of surface, an irregular border formed by massive bodies of foliage will in a great degree supply the place in landscape of moderate hills, and particularly will this be the case if it contains water in some slight depression, so situated as to double these masses."[9] The northern half of Washington Park could be laid out as one hundred acres of open turf to create the largest open space designed for parades and games anywhere in the United States.

Olmsted and Vaux believed that the only real distinction of the South Park landscape was its frontage on Lake Michigan. Yet the "grandeur" of the lake fully compensated in their eyes for the "absence of sublime or picturesque elevations of land."[10] To extend the scenic influence of the lake, they proposed cutting channels through the beach in Jackson Park, which was then nothing more than a series of marshy sandbars, so that the swampy water could flow out. Then they could dredge the area, heaping up the sand and mud on the banks high enough so that sizeable trees could grow there. From the lagoons thereby created, they planned to dredge right down the center of Midway Plaisance and connect Jackson Park with Washington Park. The result would be not only aesthetically pleasing but socially useful. Raising the level of the ground above water level would make trees, shrubs, and gardens possible. And the draining of the shore region would also contribute to the greater healthfulness of the neighborhood surrounding South Park and make it a superior residential area.

Five months after Olmsted and Vaux submitted their plan to the South Park Commissioners in March 1871, the Great Fire swept through Chicago. Although the South Park site was untouched, all work on the park was temporarily suspended and all employees except a small police force were discharged. When the project was resumed nearly a year later, it was no longer directly under the supervision of Olmsted and Vaux but of Horace W. S. Cleveland, who followed the original design as far as city finances permitted but was not allowed to make extensive alterations in the natural surface of the site. Thus the waterways joining Jackson and Washington Parks were not constructed, and only the inland part of South Park was developed. Eventually the undeveloped lakeside area became the site of the great Chicago fair, the World's Columbian Exposition of 1893, and afterward truly became Jackson Park, following Olmsted's basic design of years before.

Parks for Buffalo

In 1868, Olmsted entered into negotiations with William Dorsheimer of Buffalo about a major park project there. Unlike New York City, Buffalo had, from its beginning, experienced the advantage of good city planning. It had been laid out by Joseph Ellicott, the brother of L'Enfant's successor as planner of Washington, D.C., and was very much influenced by the L'Enfant plan for the capital city. Converging on Niagara Square, a classic square dating from the earliest period of the city, were radiating diagonal boulevards that led into street systems conforming to the local topography.

Dorsheimer and other civic-minded officials, immensely proud of a city that was growing tremendously in the latter half of the nineteenth century, were eager to have the amenities other large cities were developing. As the population of Buffalo expanded, however, they became concerned about the haphazard settlements springing up in unattractive surroundings on the outskirts of the city. Olmsted was initially invited to visit Buffalo to give his advice and to help select a rural park site. In driving about the countryside northeast of the city with Dorsheimer one Sunday afternoon, he discarded several suggestions involving land too expensive to transform into the desired pleasure ground. But coming to an elevation commanding an extended view of the city, he exclaimed, after a moment's pause, "Here is your park, almost ready made."[11]

The site, which was to become Delaware Park, consisted of rolling farm land traversed by a creek that Olmsted's expert eye realized could be easily dammed to create a large lake. The area was close enough to the city to be easily accessible, yet had not yet been laid out in streets. Dorsheimer gave Olmsted full backing and gathered together a group of community leaders, presided over by former President Millard Fillmore, before whom the designer could describe the site he had chosen and explain the advantages of a large rural park for Buffalo. In due course, the recommended land was acquired, and Olmsted's general plan was accepted.

The 350-acre Delaware Park, laid out with diverse facilities and wide areas of lakeside and meadow, was just the beginning of the work Olmsted did for Buffalo. He went on to design a whole 600-acre park system that gave the city, in the decades from the 1870s to World War I, a green and spacious serenity unexcelled anywhere in the country. Two miles nearer to town than Delaware Park, on a low bluff above Lake Erie, he created a park called the Front, with a magnificent view over the lake and the Niagara River to the Canadian shore. Across the city to the east, he developed another park, called the Parade, providing level ground for games and military displays. Throughout the city he scattered eight more squares and miscellaneous areas. Finally, to link the parks with one another and permit direct and pleasant passage between the various sections of Buffalo, he designed seven miles of parkways, bordered with turf and planted with shade trees, that provided the kind of landscape framework he had tried, unsuccessfully, to carry out in Brooklyn.

In addition, Olmsted was involved in several collaborations with H. H. Richardson in Buffalo. Richardson designed the buildings for a state hospital for the insane bordering on Delaware Park, and Olmsted planned the grounds and helped in the proper siting of the structures. They also worked together at making Niagara Square even more distinctive as a focal open space in the park network. Olmsted again was responsible for shaping and planting the grounds, while Richardson designed the formal, monumental arch.

The interconnected Buffalo park system is a good example of the kind of effective city planning Olmsted could do, given sufficient freedom to carry out his ideas. He could have done even more for the city had his recommendations for a large lakeside park at the south end of Buffalo been followed in 1888. He foresaw the need for increased waterfront development of Lake Erie, including extensive beaches and also places for the type of active sports he hoped would be accommodated otherwise than by alterations in the pastoral character of Delaware Park. The compromise inland site on which the present South Park was eventually constructed proved to be a poor choice because the southern areas of the city were allowed to grow without adequate recourse to the waterfront.

Parks for Montreal and Detroit

In 1874, Olmsted was engaged by the park commissioners of Montreal to plan and supervise the building of a park for that Canadian city over 200 years old. The experience proved to be frustrating and difficult for him in many ways. To begin with, the site of the proposed Mount Royal Park, a mass of traprock a mile long and half a mile wide, presented unusual problems. The so-called mountain was really only a hill 735 feet high on which the Montreal City Council had assembled various parcels of land totaling about 430 acres. Olmsted warned the commissioners in his earliest report that it was a most unlikely place for a park.

But the main trouble involved the commissioners themselves, who did not constitute a separate body but were merely those members of the elected common council delegated to handle park affairs. As a result, they lacked the requisite knowledge and skill that Olmsted had found in park commissioners in Brooklyn and Buffalo. He was accustomed to methodical planning and always required a topographical map of a site before he proceeded with a landscape design. The commissioners were several months late in supplying this map, but in the meantime they urged him to design a carriage road to the top of the mountain because they had to provide jobs for the city's unemployed and also to demonstrate some visible progress in the development of the new park. Then, when the map finally reached him, he learned that certain property that he had been led to believe was to be included within the boundaries of the park was, in fact, not even owned by the city and had to be excluded. By May 1876, he had redesigned the park plan three times to adapt it to changing information.

Work on Mount Royal Park continued for a number of years in fits and starts. As Olmsted got into the project, he became increasingly convinced that the apparent defects in the site could be turned into assets. For what he considered its eight distinct topographical areas, he selected romantic names to suggest their special characteristics: the crags, the most dramatic part of the site, especially when seen from the city, east of the mountain; the upperfell, located just above the crags; the brackenfell, lower down and south of the crags; the underfell, immediately below the crags; the glades, a long, gentle, protected depression of the surface; the cragsfoot, just below the crags; and the piedmont and côte placide, containing rough rolling ground that grew smoother as one went north and east.[12]

Each of these topographical divisions he proposed to treat as its natural character suggested, but he was also determined to evoke what he considered the essential genius of the mountain and to let his park design evolve from that. He would make the mountain look taller, more "mountainous," by making the high parts seem higher, the low parts lower. The one great asset of Mount Royal was its charming natural scenery, and he became enthusiastic about the idea that no other city in the world possessed a site with such potential for the development of its scenery. He cautioned that it would be spoiled by the introduction of "ribband-gardening, floral embroidery, sub-tropical borders, and whatever is commonly found on a polished lawn of the present fashion."[13] He preferred retaining, as much as possible, the natural scenery: "The very best things for your purpose are such as, once established and a little guarded, will take care of themselves, propagate and spread, like our common American wild flowers."[14]

In no other park reports that Olmsted ever wrote did he try so hard to convey the metaphysical experience that a rural park provided for him and, by extension, for all those citizens who would partake of it. Perhaps it was the distinctive mountain scenery of Mount Royal in particular that made him attempt to describe the experience in poetic terms in a way he had never done before. Opposite the preface to a pamphlet he wrote on the project in 1881, he set down brief quotations from William Wordsworth, John Ruskin, Francis Bacon, and James Russell Lowell as literary expressions of what he considered to be the meaning of his art.

Olmsted appreciated the panoramic views from the summit of Mount Royal, but he deplored the modern entrepreneurial tendency "to whisk people up to the highest eminence of the mountain, give them a big mouthful of landscape beauty, and slide them back to town in the shortest possible way."[15] What he appreciated most was the gradual experience of ascending or descending the mountain, the soothing and refreshing influence of the natural scenery when enjoyed "as successive incidents of a sustained landscape poem, to each of which the mind is gradually and sweetly led up, and from which it is gradually and sweetly led away, so that they become a part of a consistent experience."[16] For this reason, his plan called for carriage roads that gradually wended their way up the side of Mount Royal through leafy tunnels offering occasional glimpses of the surrounding countryside. These roads should look as natural as possible, the topography dictating the routes.

On numerous occasions Olmsted attempted to explain to the commissioners and to other citizens of Montreal the rationale behind his design. In September 1877, for example, a public meeting was held but was largely unproductive, he felt, in educating public opinion. It proved difficult to convey his metaphysical and poetic enthusiasm to a public that included many who believed that the park he described was a needless luxury. In 1881, he tried again to communicate his ideas in a long pamphlet intended primarily for the park commissioners. The job to be done, he kept insisting, must be regarded as a unified work of art, and the essential purpose of the park—providing charming scenery—should be kept in mind whenever even the most minor decision was being made.

Although Olmsted was never able to get the Montreal commissioners to understand fully his idealistic purpose, he could also be a realist when he had to. After he finally realized that they could not be persuaded to see things his way, he capitulated to their conditions and adapted his park design accordingly. Because he was forced to make the grades up the mountain slope steeper than he would have liked, he had great difficulty in designing satisfactory carriage entrances to the park. He had repeatedly urged the city fathers to acquire more property than they immediately needed, on the assumption that land values around the park would appreciate dramatically once it was completed. But his previous experiences, particularly in New York City, had taught him it was unlikely that park commissioners could be persuaded to adopt such a philosophy. Nevertheless, after all his painstaking efforts, he did eventually succeed to a remarkable extent in creating a park consonant with his basic conception.

During the latter part of his career, Olmsted was also engaged in a number of smaller public park projects such as Belle Isle Park in Detroit. When Belle Isle, a low-lying island in the narrow Detroit River, was set aside as a park in 1881, he came out to survey the land and prepare a plan. Since the island was no more than half a mile downstream from the business center of Detroit, he was able to combine some of the attractions of a suburban waterside resort, approached by steam ferry, with those of a regular urban park. Canals were cut through the soggy ground, and roadways were built up with material from these canals. He designed a formal area toward the end of the island nearest the city and also provided a natural forest carefully pruned so that sun could penetrate to the undergrowth.

Park Work for Boston

Olmsted's park work in Boston has proved to be just as important, both technically and historically, as his work in New York. The idea of a rural park for Boston went back at least as far as the 1850s, but it was not until 1867 that he was first called in for professional advice by Professor Charles Eliot Norton of Harvard. At that time Boston possessed no major parks except the Common, going back to 1634, and the later Public Garden. In February 1870, Olmsted read a paper, "Public Parks and the Enlargement of Towns," before the American Social Science Association at the Lowell Institute in Boston. This paper was the most detailed explanation he ever gave of his views on the planning of cities.

He felt keenly the changes that had occurred in the United States since he was a boy growing up in rural and small-town Connecticut. He had originally chosen the life of the farmer as the proper one for a civilized man with a scientific bent. But that life had proved impracticable for him, and so, beginning to realize that cities would be the centers of the future, he had moved to the city, which came to symbolize for him mankind's historic social progress. He found an "intimate connection" between the growth of cities and the "dying out of slavery and feudal customs, of priestcraft and government by divine right, the multiplication of books, newspapers, schools, and other means of popular education and the adoption of improved methods of communication, transportation, and of various labor-saving inventions."[17]

Olmsted predicted that cities would continue to grow as human progress continued. He recognized the rising rate of social problems caused by the closer proximity of people, noting in particular the increase in crime, alcoholism, prostitution, and mental and emotional disorders. Yet he also took the characteristically idealistic view of his generation that "modern science has beyond all question determined many of the causes of the special evils by which men are afflicted in towns, and placed means in our hands for guarding against them."[18] One of his principal planning goals was to create an environment that would afford calm recreation and be conducive to a healthy state of mind. For him, rural parks were a powerful counterbalance to the "devouring eagerness and intellectual strife" of city life.[19] From his experiences in park building thus far, he was convinced that such parks were great civilizing forces influencing the minds of men through their imaginations. They were also great democratizing experiences, giving people of all classes the opportunity to mingle together.

Then, addressing himself specifically to his Boston audience, Olmsted pointed out that Boston was certain to grow tremendously in the future. There was no reason, however, for the newer residential areas of the city to spring up haphazardly as had happened with the often congested and noisy older downtown commercial areas. Careful planning was required, including provision for a rural park that

he described as a "simple, broad, open space of clean greensward" to
shut out the city completely from the landscape and to provide
needed recreation.[20] He concluded by saying that the question of
the site and boundaries of such a park demanded much more
serious attention than was frequently given to problems of municipal interest.

Olmsted's address before the American Social Science Association
was afterward widely circulated as a pamphlet. A park bill for
Boston was passed by the Massachusetts state legislature at about
the same time but failed to receive the necessary two-thirds majority
in the election of November 1870. Olmsted was not unduly discouraged. "Better wait a few years," he advised, "than adopt a narrow local scheme."[21] As it happened, it was five years before the
park bill was accepted by popular vote. In the meantime, he was engaged in a work that would eventually form part of the Boston park
system. Charles Sprague Sargent asked him to help design the new
Arnold Arboretum in Boston. Harvard College actually owned the
grounds of the Arboretum, but Sargent wanted them to be incorporated into the Boston park system. The condition was that the
city, while spending the money to lay out the grounds, would agree
to leave the planting in Sargent's hands so that scientific experi-
ments could be carried out. At first, President Eliot of Harvard and
the Boston city authorities were cool to the plan, but eventually the
Arboretum was in fact incorporated into the park system. To further that end, Olmsted suggested a clever legal arrangement that
went into effect in 1882. Today this combination of the scientific
and the recreational worked out by Olmsted and Sargent is world-
renowned.

Even though the Boston park bill was passed in 1875, the city
council delayed voting appropriations for the acquisition of land.
Late in 1875, however, the park commissioners asked Olmsted's advice on areas to be considered as possible park sites. After careful
field inspections, he formulated definite ideas about a whole new
park system for Boston and recommended immediate approval of
specific areas along the Charles River, in the marshy Back Bay,
around Jamaica Pond, and in West Roxbury. But it was not until

1877 that the city council, finally reacting to public pressure, authorized the acquisition of land and the laying out of a park in the unimproved portion of the Back Bay.

Olmsted realized at once that, before any park work could begin, a severe drainage problem in the Back Bay area would have to be solved. The Back Bay Fens was a noxious tidal swamp and creek left over from the time when all of the Back Bay was a shallow body of salt water. Its sewage and swamp water created a serious health problem as well as a foul stench. Equally important was the matter of flood control. Emptying into the Back Bay were two streams that drained several thousands of surrounding acres and that tended to flood badly when heavy rains and high tides backed up in the tidal basin of the Charles River. The flooding and tidal fluctuations had to be eliminated.

But Olmsted had done his usual careful spadework. He ingeniously devised a plan that would transform the Back Bay area, or the Fens, as he preferred to call it, into a public park and would, at the same time, solve the drainage problem. His first technical innovation was to control the amount of water in the Back Bay by building tide gates where the Fens flowed into the Charles. He next proceeded to bury a huge sewage interceptor on the Boston side of the Fens basin. This conduit reduced health hazards and provided a run-off for one of the two streams. In times of extremely heavy rains, he anticipated that the Fens parkland would serve as a temporary storage basin for run-off water without permanent damage to its vegetation. His final preliminary work was filling in the land around this conduit.[22]

Olmsted's plan—one of the most elaborate technical feats of his career—was a brilliant combination of practicality and creative imagination. And his design for the park itself was equally successful, though, because of inadequate annual appropriations, the project took a long time to complete. Codgrass was cultivated on the submerged mud flats, and trees were planted around the rim. From six entrances, visitors discovered park drives, paths for strolling, and the beginning of what was intended to be an extensive bridle path system that Olmsted named the Ride. Since the channels of the waterway were relatively narrow and winding, water traffic was limited to canoes. Native waterfowl in extraordinary numbers occupied the Fens even while the dredging was being done and became a permanent aquatic feature.

While working on the Fens in 1879–80, Olmsted began entertaining the possibility of continuing a strip of parkland up the valley of the Muddy River, one of the two streams emptying into Back Bay, all the way to Jamaica Pond, one of the park sites he had previously recommended. The park commissioners realized the value of his idea, and their next annual report included a preliminary plan by Olmsted. Construction was not to begin for ten years, but here was a vital link in the famous seven-mile "emerald necklace" that Olmsted was eventually to stretch from Boston Common around the circumference of the city all the way to West Roxbury Park in Dorchester.

Franklin Park and the Boston Greenbelt Plan

West Roxbury Park was another park site that he had already recommended. In 1881, the city council finally authorized the park commissioners to begin acquiring the 500 acres for it. Since the site was in a region of suburban and rural residences, the process of obtaining the property was lengthy. By the time Olmsted had prepared his final design in 1885, the name of the park had been officially changed to Franklin Park as a memorial to Benjamin Franklin. One of Boston's most illustrious sons, Franklin had set up in his will a fund that, after a century's accumulation, was used for the purchase of the park.

Franklin Park ranks alongside Central and Prospect parks as one of Olmsted's greatest achievements in rural park design. The topography, partly wooded and partly pasture, afforded superb picturesque scenery. Olmsted himself thought the park could be compared favorably with Fontainebleau, outside Paris, for its landscape distance, intricacy, and mystery. It is about the same overall size as Prospect Park but chunkier in dimensions. At its core is a large central space from which a relatively level meadow, called the Playstead, once led off to the north. A curving space called Ellicottdale would draw the visitor toward the northwest. Between the two was the forward thrust of Schoolmaster Hill. On the west side of the central space was Scarboro Hill, with the idyllic Scarboro Pond lying south of it. On the east side of the park, surrounded by woods, was an architectonically formal space, originally called the Greeting, that corresponded to the Mall in Central Park. A circuit drive wound around the park just inside the belt of woods of varying width that was so important, for Olmsted, in screening out the city. The park contained some six miles of driveways, thirteen miles of walks, and two miles of bridle paths.[23]

On the face of his plan for Franklin Park, Olmsted specified that the larger part of the property, a mile long and three quarters of a mile wide, which he designated the "Country Park," should be set

Franklin Park: Photograph of Ellicottdale in Franklin Park, Boston, at the turn of the century, with tennis courts marked out on the grass. (Courtesy of Olmsted Associates, Inc., and the Frances Loeb Library, Harvard Graduate School of Design)

apart with absolute exclusiveness for the quiet enjoyment of natural scenery. Yet, by the time he designed this park, he was also responding more flexibly than in his previous parks to the growing demand for active recreation. Thus, around this rural core, he not only provided excellent fields for such lawn sports as tennis and croquet but also introduced ball diamonds and other spaces for boys' and men's athletics.

Today almost the whole open space in the park is a heavily played municipal golf course. The entire northern meadow, formerly the Playstead, has become a stadium and parking lot. This particular area has therefore been lost completely in terms of park value. The main open spaces that remain are now used as a cross-country course by Boston colleges.[24] Yet, despite the sad neglect and the various encroachments to which Franklin Park has been subjected, even now ample evidence remains of Olmsted's creativity. Although it is no longer the country park he planned, a largely rural atmosphere still prevails.

Not until 1890 was the grading of the banks for the Muddy River improvement begun. The delay was caused in part by the fact that the town of Brookline had to concur in the purchase of land for the project because the boundary between the two municipalities ran largely along the middle of the stream.[25] Yet the success of the entire "emerald necklace" depended on this connecting link between the Back Bay Fens and Muddy River. Eventually, an agreement was worked out, and the "green fingers" project, an attempt to interlace an essentially urban complex with parklike corridors of the surrounding countryside, became widely admired.

Three years before, the park commissioners had voted to apply the name "Parkway" to the entire seven-mile continuous linkage of parks, which was to extend in a wide semicircle around the city. They thereby fully endorsed what Olmsted had conceived and proposed some years before as the "Promenade." The Parkway would begin with Boston Common and the Public Garden in the heart of the city. From there, Commonwealth Avenue, a handsome, tree-lined esplanade, would lead directly to the Back Bay Fens. From the Fens the route would follow the course of the Muddy River upstream, first northwest, then making a ninety-degree turn south-west to a large cattail swamp that would be converted into Leverett Pond. From there the Parkway would continue to Jamaica Pond. Beyond that, a park strip called the Arborway would be added, joining Jamaica Pond with the Arnold Arboretum and with an entrance to Franklin Park.

This whole Boston greenbelt plan, following topography and residential growth from city to suburb, was the boldest and most comprehensive that Olmsted ever devised. The basic concept may have been inherent in the dreaming that he and Vaux had done about the New York of the future, in which Central and Prospect parks would be but the first phase of a complete system of pleasure grounds and parkways linking the greater metropolitan region. But in Boston Olmsted was actually able to design a park system that became the standard by which future park systems would be judged. He established a hierarchy of features incorporated into many of these later systems: a large rural park; medium-size parks for relaxation and picnicking; smaller landscaped areas with ponds for recreation; linear parkland for pleasure drives, riding, and hiking. His sketches of circulation patterns, though not fully carried out even in Boston, provided for a separation of traffic into distinct lanes: sidewalks and streets for access to houses; promenades for casual strollers; carriageways; and saddle paths for horseback riders. These parkways, carefully planted with shade trees, would serve the "triple purposes of delight, recreation, and circulation" of traffic.[26]

Olmsted's work on the Boston park system proved generally to be a pleasant relief from the frustrations and strains of his work in New York City during the Gilded Age. The social and political environment was entirely different in Boston, which had not yet been torn apart by the factional strife that had made working on Central Park so difficult. He was no longer in a subordinate's role, as he had frequently felt himself to be in New York, and he could insist on administrative arrangements to protect his authority against political intrusions. Such intrusions proved to be rare, and his park planning benefited directly from the support of the Boston Brahmins, who were usually sympathetic to his aims.[27]

In 1895, the year Olmsted retired after forty years of professional practice, work on the Muddy River section and on Leverett Park was basically complete, and Jamaica Park was in its final stages. As a tribute to him, the park commissioners voted in 1900 that what had formerly been known as Leverett and Jamaica parks should be renamed Olmsted Park.[28] After his retirement the Olmsted firm in Brookline continued his ideals for many decades. He had taken his stepson John Charles Olmsted into full partnership in 1884, and in 1893 Charles Eliot returned to the firm in which he had served as apprentice. The firm became Olmsted, Olmsted, and Eliot. By the time of Eliot's return, he had already earned a name for himself as a talented landscape architect.

During the 1890s Eliot followed Olmsted's lead in advocating the public preservation of natural areas out beyond city boundaries as scenic and recreational resources for people closely bound to urban areas. He was influential in the creation of the Boston region's Metropolitan Park Commission, which acted to extend the Boston park system to include the Blue Hills Reservation, the Middlesex Fells, Revere Beach, and other open land. When Eliot joined the Olmsteds, the firm was officially appointed landscape architects to the permanent Metropolitan Park Commission.

It was only natural that Frederick Olmsted should take great pride in having his firm involved in the first metropolitan system of parks in the United States. He recognized the full significance of Boston's regional undertaking, both in terms of the development of its suburbs and in terms of the standing of his firm and his profession. In 1893, he urged his partners to concentrate their best energies on the completion of both metropolitan and city projects in Boston. In their potential historical and educational impact, they were, he declared, "the most important work of our profession now in hand anywhere in the world."[29] He thus foresaw that the Boston park work would be as influential in general suburban improvement as Central Park had already been in urban park development.

Chapter Five

Campus and Institutional Designs

Campus Plan for Berkeley

Olmsted's introduction to the planning of college and university campuses came relatively early in his career as landscape architect but proved unusually frustrating in those years. While he was in California as superintendent of the Mariposa Estate, the newly organized College of California, later to be called Berkeley, was being planned in a location across the bay from San Francisco, a few miles north of the town of Oakland. In March 1864, the trustees, having heard of Olmsted's reputation, asked his advice on laying out the property. He began crossing over periodically by ferry, even sleepng out at least once on the proposed grounds to determine whether the climate there might be milder than that of San Francisco. He became convinced that it was.

The idea of planning campuses as large, unified groups of buildings had existed in the United States since before the Revolution, but Olmsted's plan for Berkeley, though never actually carried out, may be said to be the first campus design by a landscape architect. Furthermore, what he proposed was not just a college campus but a combination of campus, residential development, and park. He thus had his first opportunity—even before the suburb of Riverside, Illinois—to plan the arrangement of a total community from its very inception.

Before his return to New York City, Olmsted worked on a preliminary study of the placement of buildings, visualizing in his mind's eye the trees and shrubs that should clothe the sparsely shaded hills around what would become the college center. In 1866, after his return east, he completed a full report that, like many of the reports he wrote throughout his career, suggested a specific plan only after setting forth the principles on which he felt the profession of landscape architecture rested. He was concerned with building upon solid philosophical truths about the way man could function optimally in society. With Berkeley, the emphasis was on the ideal of the total community, of which the proposed college was the center and raison d'être.

Olmsted reasoned that students at Berkeley would have access to the cultural opportunities of San Francisco and yet not be constantly distracted from their studies. He rejected the monastic seclusion of the medieval universities. Since "scholars should be prepared to lead, not to follow reluctantly after, the advancing line of civilization," they should be "surrounded by manifestations of refined domestic life, these being unquestionably the ripest and best fruits of civilization."[1] Thus he urged creating a neighborhood of attractive homes in the vicinity of the principal college buildings. Here the professors and their families would live. This congenial nucleus would also be likely to attract cultivated San Franciscans who would welcome the opportunity to establish suburban residences in an academic environment unsurpassed in the region for climate, soil, foliage, water supply, and scenic views.

Although the street plans of the new towns in the West were customarily constructed on the rectangular grid system, Olmsted followed the picturesque style that he and Vaux had used in Central Park rather than a formal, symmetrical arrangement. In designing gently winding roads, he would be utilizing the natural topography of the land and giving property owners the best landscape effects possible from the largest number of vantage points. But he was also interested in discouraging from the immediate residential area as much commercial traffic as possible. The roads would be laid out so as to afford moderately direct access between the different parts of the neighborhood but to be inconvenient for through traffic.

With regard to the campus itself, Olmsted intended that the central academic buildings be placed on an artificial plateau at the head of a dell between two hills, with an unrestricted outlook westward over the Pacific. He planned two large structures for a start. One, built of brick, stone, and iron, would house the library, college records, and scientific collections. The other would contain an assembly hall, classrooms, and faculty offices. He wanted students at Berkeley to benefit from the nearby residential community. They would therefore live not in large dormitory complexes, but either with private families or in buildings having the general appearance of large private residences with living and dining facilities for from twenty to forty students.[2]

Plans for Agricultural Colleges

Olmsted's detailed plan for Berkeley was never adopted and was, in time, even lost. His accompanying report, which did survive, was used only in an advisory way by William Hammond Hall, who was put in charge of the actual development of the new university campus in 1874. Nor did Olmsted fare any better with the reports he wrote for the trustees of both the Massachusetts and the Maine agricultural colleges. In 1866, the same year in which he wrote his report on Berkeley, Henry F. French, president of the Massachusetts Agricultural College at Amherst, wrote asking his advice about planning the college grounds. This was one of the land-grant colleges organized under the Morrill Act of 1862, which gave to every state and territory thirty thousand acres of public land for each of its senators and representatives. The proceeds from the sale of this land were to be used for education in the practical sciences related to agriculture and mechanics.

As an adviser to the newly founded magazine the *Nation*, Olmsted had already pondered the problems of these new agricultural colleges and was soon prepared to offer his philosophy as well as a landscaping solution. His report urged that the Massachusetts Agricultural College should do more than facilitate instruction and demonstrations in farming. It should also influence the habits of its students and prepare them to exercise their rights and duties as citizens and householders. Olmsted held the conviction that farmers had the same civic responsibilities and could even learn to enjoy much the same intellectual pursuits as professional men and should be educated to this end. To slow down the much deplored tendency of young people to leave the farms for the cities, an agricultural college ought to demonstrate ways of reducing the special disadvantage of farm life, its social seclusion. Thus the new college buildings should be placed within easy reach of nearby homes, community center, post office, and railway station in order to carry out the idea of a rural neighborhood. Once more, as he had done in his plan for Berkeley, he stressed the ideal of the total community. For the Amherst campus, he did not specify that each residential building ought to resemble a large family home but only that each should be related to the others to approximate the buildings in a rural community.[3]

President French was pleased with Olmsted's report, but the trustees could not agree on it. Eventually the president resigned out of frustration over the project. The report, however, made a good impression elsewhere. Both the *Nation* and the *North American Review* commented on it favorably, several agricultural journals and daily papers praised it, and many advocates of independent land-grant colleges endorsed it enthusiastically. Among these were the trustees of the proposed Maine Agricultural College, who invited Olmsted to travel to Orono and advise them on laying out a campus. The bill establishing the Maine college was the work of Phineas Barnes, later its first president, and demonstrated Barnes's familiarity with Olmsted's ideas by stipulating that the "internal organization of the college shall be on the plan of one or more well-regulated households and families, so that the students may be brought into relations of domestic intimacy and confidence with their teachers."[4]

Olmsted inspected the property and wrote a formal report in 1867, including a number of features he had already suggested in his

Berkeley and Amherst proposals. Again he emphasized the importance of the total environment in the life of the student. In contrast to the formal pattern of English universities like Oxford and Cambridge, with their large stone buildings, he favored small, detached structures made of wood, models of "healthy, cheerful, convenient family homes." The arrangement of buildings to form a rural village would accustom students of an environment that would probably surround them in their later lives. In designing classrooms, he anticipated modern educational practices by recommending movable partitions to permit maximum use of space and also to provide for future additions to the buildings.[5]

The Morrill Act of 1862, passed during the Civil War, had included a provision for the compulsory military training of civilians in the new land-grant colleges. In his report Olmsted took this training into account. During the Civil War he had noted the widespread ignorance shown by the volunteer officers in obtaining adequate food, shelter, and sanitation for their men. Therefore, at Maine, he recommended forming the students into companies of forty. Each company would have its commissary officer, storeroom, kitchen, and mess room, and each student in turn would undertake for his company the duties of commissary officer. This kind of environment, Olmsted believed, would nurture enlightened leaders.[6] Once more, however, his plans were to be unrealized. A new board of trustees elected later in 1867 decided that his report put too much emphasis on the military. None of his recommendations, in fact, was followed.

Campus and other Institutional Designs

The first of Olmsted's campus projects that reached fruition during the late 1860s was the Columbia Institution for the Deaf and Dumb, later to be known as Gallaudet College, in Washington, D.C. In 1866, Edward M. Gallaudet, who had been a childhood friend of Olmsted, asked him to improve the grounds of the school, located in the open countryside northeast of the national capital.

Olmsted was extremely pleased to be able to create a beautiful and humane setting for the education of the deaf. He took pains to ensure that the senses of sight and smell would be gratified as fully as possible and provided facilities for the study of botany, ornamental gardening, and rural architecture. Vaux was brought in to design several of the buildings.

The following year Olmsted made several trips to Ithaca, New York, to study a plan already designed for the grounds of the new Cornell University. The first president, Andrew D. White, liked his suggestions and regretted that the school could not act to replace its one big building with the smaller ones proposed by Olmsted before its official opening in 1868. College officials continued, however, to consult him about buildings, grounds, and academic matters. In 1873, when Ezra Cornell was charged with fraud in connection with the sale of the college's land grant, Olmsted became a trustee for a short time to show his support.[7] Thus, while the advice he gave over a period of years was not evident in many concrete details on campus, his informal influence as Cornell's first landscape adviser had considerable effect.

Beginning in the 1870s, and throughout the rest of his career, Olmsted was also involved in the campus planning of a number and variety of other educational institutions, including Amherst, Trinity, Yale, Johns Hopkins, Colgate, Union, the University of Vermont, Smith, Harvard, Stanford, the United States Military Academy, Columbia, Princeton, Lawrenceville School, Groton School, and Washington University, St. Louis. He was also engaged in a wide variety of other institutional designs, including the Massachusetts General Hospital in Boston, Oakwood Cemetery in Syracuse, the Hartford Retreat for the Insane, the Schuylkill Arsenal in Philadelphia, the McLean Asylum in Waverly, Massachusetts, the Connecticut State Capitol in Hartford, and the state capitol grounds, Montgomery, Alabama. In addition, in collaboration with H. H. Richardson, he designed the Buffalo State Asylum, Crane Memorial Library at Quincy, Massachusetts, Converse Memorial Library at Malden, Massachusetts, the library, station, and Ames Memorial

Hall at North Easton, Massachusetts, and a number of suburban stations along the line of the Boston and Albany Railroad.

Capitol Project: Albany, New York

During the 1870s and 1880s Olmsted was much absorbed in two large capitol projects, one in Albany, New York, the other in Washington, D.C. The new state capitol at Albany, begun in 1867, was based on an Italian Renaissance design by Thomas S. Fuller. Originally budgeted at four million dollars, it had by the mid-seventies already cost five million and was only two stories above ground. Both the cost and the appropriateness of the design itself came under such criticism that the state legislature appointed a new capitol commission, chaired by Lieutenant Governor William Dorsheimer, who was already the friend and patron of Olmsted and Richardson. Dorsheimer named as an advisory board to the commission these two men and, in addition, Leopold Eidlitz, a distinguished New York City architect. Olmsted was selected along with the two architects not only because of his reputation as a landscape architect but because of his administrative experience with large public works.[8]

In 1876, the advisory board submitted to Dorsheimer's commission a polite but critical report, of which Olmsted was chief author. The board uncovered no gross fraud and admitted that the cost of the building so far had not been excessive. It found the site ill chosen for a monumental building but felt it unthinkable to tear down five million dollars' worth of construction: the essential faults of the original design would therefore be permanently fastened on the building. But in a surprising break with aesthetic convention, the board proposed to complete the work by abandoning the Renaissance style and adopting the Romanesque. Features of the already completed stories could be modified to make the transition as harmonious as possible. Only a radical change, the board concluded, could redeem the capitol, lending coherence and dignity where none existed in the original Renaissance plan.[9]

While initial public reaction to the advisory board's report was favorable, the combining of the two styles offended a number of leading architects such as Richard Morris Hunt, James Renwick, and Richard Upjohn in an age when Renaissance and Gothic architecture was very much in fashion. Vociferous and sometimes savage attacks and counterattacks were exchanged over the new plans that Richardson and Eidlitz had drawn up. Olmsted rushed into print to defend himself and his colleagues. Thus work on the Albany capitol was marked by further controversy and delay. After some revisions, however, the board's plans were finally accepted, and the three men were charged with overseeing the completion of the costly building and its grounds. Olmsted's responsibility was no longer limited to landscape work at this point; all three men were engaged jointly in the whole project.[10]

Ultimately, despite the critical brouhaha, their design was largely vindicated, although the finished capitol was never completely satisfactory even to its designers because of the element of patchwork. Olmsted believed afterward that what could be done had been done decently. He especially liked the richness of detail in the Senate chamber, for which Richardson had designed a great free-standing clock. At the time of the gala opening of the still-unfinished building in 1879, the *American Architect and Building News* declared that, although the new capitol might lack the unity of a harmonious whole, "we have a work of vigor, individuality and artistic power which, in spite of a forced conformity to an original scheme that does not suit with it, and that involves many shortcomings in the final result, will give it a place of permanent honor."[11]

Capitol Project: Washington, D.C.

More satisfying to Olmsted was the capitol project in Washington, D.C. In 1873, Senator Justin Morrill, author of the land-grant bill and chairman of the Senate Committee on Public Grounds, invited Olmsted to Washington to discuss landscaping the recently enlarged grounds of the Capitol. The Capitol building had, from the time it was first planned, been in the hands of capable architects, but the grounds, now amounting to about fifty acres, had never been adequately improved: they provided a shabby setting for a majestic formal structure. After Congress appropriated two hundred thousand dollars the following year, Olmsted was officially appointed landscape architect to the United States Capitol.

He was accustomed to take the larger view of any new project he undertook. After having thoroughly surveyed the grounds, he urgently recommended that they should not be considered separately but in conjunction with all contiguous public grounds reaching as far as the White House. He argued that if the government buildings on these grounds—occupied at this time by the State, Justice, Treasury, War, Navy, and Agriculture departments and the Smithsonian Institution—were treated as a single field of landscape, a sustained and impressive "federal bond" would be created, symbolizing the capital of the union.[12] Congress, however, was not receptive to this grand scheme, and Olmsted had to proceed with plans for the Capitol grounds only.

He recognized that his design would have to facilitate the business of Congress by making the Capitol easily accessible from the twenty-one city streets leading into its grounds. He also had to set off the great national monument handsomely and keep it the dominant feature in the plan. He provided a total of forty-six pedestrian and carriage entrances into the grounds. To offset the large amount of paving required to accommodate both routine congressional traffic and many tourists, he arranged trees and shrubbery to achieve a general impression of restfulness and shade. It was especially important that the grounds be attractive and cool in Washington's summer humidity. To achieve this end, Olmsted used low, thickly branching trees that shut out the sun but permitted a good view of the Capitol. The plantings were displayed not so much for their individual distinctions as for the effect of blending in larger compositional patterns to produce the illusion of depth and distance. In places where turf would be difficult to maintain because of dense shade, he used a ground cover of creepers and low perennials that would blend the taller foliage with the verdure of the lawns and increase the sense of perspective.[13]

The unusually poor soil had to be improved to support the turf, trees, and shrubs. Some trees had to be removed and land regraded so that the Capitol could be seen properly. The operation proved to be expensive: "I should hardly like the Ways and Means to know that I meant to have $60,000 spent for the improvement of the soil," he wrote to his friend George Waring, who had worked with him on Central Park, "but I don't see how a tolerable condition can be hoped for at much less cost than that, do you?"[14] He consistently followed the policy that no section of ground was to be brought to completion unless it could be finished perfectly within its remaining congressional appropriation and before cold weather ended the outdoor working season: "Besides the general objection that premature and incomplete finish always creates misconceptions and diminishes ultimate popularity, the more chaotic the ground looks until the rougher preliminary and foundation work is out of the way, the better it will be thought of and the less will be the loss through damage and misuse of the final surfaces."[15]

The original architects of the Capitol had designed the main facade to face east, expecting that the major growth of Washington would occur in that direction. The ground to the west had been slighted despite the fact that it offered a splendid view up the Potomac Valley. But by the time of Andrew Jackson's presidency, it was clear that the principal development of the city would in fact be westward. About seven acres were added at that time to the Capitol's western slope. Thus, when Olmsted was commissioned to landscape the entire grounds, he realized the need to give the neglected west side, which was the most frequently seen, appropriate distinction.

The major problem he faced was that the western slope was too steep to allow for a grand approaching avenue. The imaginative solution he devised was a magnificent broad marble terrace placed around the north, west, and south sides of the building, and approached on the west by a double flight of marble steps. He envisioned this terrace as transforming the appearance of the building as viewed from the Mall. It would make the Capitol look larger than it was and also give it the grandeur of a base that the recently enlarged Capitol dome needed.[16]

Congress adopted Olmsted's design but subsequently deleted money for the terrace from the appropriation bill for the Capitol grounds in 1875. He was naturally disappointed but optimistically expected the appropriation to be restored the following year. It was not forthcoming until 1884, partly because some legislators feared that the vast terrace would tend to hide rather than enhance the Capitol. Then two years later, Senator Henry L. Dawes of Massachusetts suddenly proposed altering the already approved plan for the terrace by having windows installed in the walls so that the areas within could be used for occupancy instead of for storage as designed. Olmsted responded that this was not just a minor alteration but a major change in design. Enlisting the support of his friend and colleague Richardson, he spearheaded a fight against Dawes's proposal. His vigorous opposition to the windows resulted in something of a compromise: Congress permitted only the terrace wall on the west side between the stairs to be installed with windows.[17] Over the years since it was finally completed, the terrace has proved a great success and serves as further evidence that Olmsted could design in the monumental as well as in the natural style.

Campus Plan for Stanford

Olmsted's last great opportunity for campus design came in 1886 with an invitation from Senator Leland Stanford of California to plan the grounds of a university in memory of Stanford's only son, who had died of typhoid fever at the age of fifteen. A multimillionaire, Stanford had acquired seven thousand acres in the San Jose valley, thirty miles south of San Francisco. Olmsted took along to the West Coast his son Frederick and Henry Sargent Codman, then a young apprentice in his firm. Codman persuaded Olmsted to ask the unprecedented fee of ten thousand dollars for a preliminary study, and Olmsted got the amount.[18] When he visited Stanford at his Menlo Park home, he recognized what the major problem with the new client would be in a region where water was scarce:

I find Governor Stanford [formerly governor of California] bent on giving his university New England scenery, New England trees and turf,

to be obtained only by lavish use of water. The landscape of the region
is said to be fine in its way, but nobody thinks of anything in gardening
that will not be thoroughly unnatural to it. What can be done I don't
know, but it will be an interesting subject of study.[19]

At the same time, the young architect Charles A. Coolidge had
gone west to try to secure the architectural work on the campus
project for his firm, Shepley, Rutan, and Coolidge, which succeeded
to the practice of H. H. Richardson after his death that same year.
Coolidge was successful, and Olmsted found himself embarking on
another real collaboration such as he had previously had, first with
Calvert Vaux and later with Richardson. Olmsted and Coolidge
began by helping to select the exact site of the new Stanford campus.
Olmsted favored a commanding slope in the coastal range of rolling
foothills west of Palo Alto, covered with the remains of a pine and
redwood forest. The formidable Leland Stanford, however, wanted
the main college buildings placed on a large meadowlike portion of
the property where his son had spent long hours on horseback. Here
the landscape architect yielded the point, and a topographical survey
was made of the site that Stanford desired.[20]

Olmsted and Stanford were both strong-willed men, and Olmsted
was correct in sensing that their relationship would be difficult. Not
only the site but the treatment of landscape and architecture became
an issue between them. Back in Boston, Olmsted found himself
warning Stanford of precisely the danger he had foreseen: attempting to build the new university in a style inappropriate to its regional setting. The New England college campus, with its brick
Georgian architecture, broad stretches of lawn, and tree-shaded
walks, was an unsuitable model, he wrote to Stanford, because it
could not be satisfactorily recreated in California. The styles of
buildings and gardens in southern European countries like Greece,
Italy, and Spain would be more appropriate to the semiarid climate
of California than those of Harvard or Amherst.[21]

Standing firm against Leland Stanford this time, Olmsted and
Coolidge eventually persuaded him to agree to an adaptation of the

adobe buildings of California, and the final style was distinctly Californian: a blending of California mission architecture with Mediterranean-Romanesque. It also featured such Richardsonian motifs as short columns with decorated capitals, low, rounded hemisphere arches, and heavy stone walls. The one- and two-story buildings, with pitched roofs of red tile, were arranged to form arcaded quadrangles. Instead of attempting to provide green lawns, Olmsted had the quadrangles paved with stone blocks and planted with ornamental palms. He even sent Henry Codman abroad to study trees and to select plant materials from Spain and the North African coast that would flourish in Palo Alto's warm, dry climate without constant watering.

The architectural and landscape designs that Olmsted and Coolidge prepared for Stanford University were a striking departure from Olmsted's previous campus designs and represented an innovative American academic style. Partly to provide protection from rain, heat, and wind, they avoided the open arrangement of buildings then customary on college campuses and created a more closed system of small quadrangular courtyards surrounded by low, arcaded buildings. The formal arcades, adapted from Mediterranean models, were planned to afford easy and comfortable passage from one courtyard area to another and also to be conducive to sociability among students and faculty.[22] Olmsted believed that the connected but self-contained teaching units incorporated into the campus would reflect a vision of education as a number of individual disciplines joined by a common ideal. Another novel feature of the plan was providing a clear pattern for the future linear expansion of Stanford in harmony with the original design. Olmsted did not expect that the university would build on all of its available land at once but wanted to insure that all future academic and residential growth would be integrated by axial systems around the central quadrangle.[23]

When Olmsted and Coolidge submitted the final designs and model to Stanford for approval in 1887, he insisted on several alterations such as a large memorial arch and a sweeping approach at the main entrance in place of the modest, understated entrance that they felt was more in keeping with the rest of the plan. In general, however, Olmsted was able to get along reasonably well with Stanford until 1890.[24] He directed the basic plan of the university while it was under construction, traveling several times to California and sending Codman when he himself could not go. He also planned a railroad station and the residential community that became Palo Alto, and he superintended the engineering of the roads of both the university and the proposed town.[25]

Olmsted had his heart set on beginning a reforestation project in the hills above the university. He especially wanted to establish on their lower slopes an arboretum containing samples of all the trees of California, and also of trees from other parts of the world appropriate to the local climate. He had already employed a Scottish forester, Thomas H. Douglas, to supervise the planting on campus. Douglas was instructed to set up an experimental nursery and to keep a detailed record of every tree on the grounds. But Leland Stanford could not seem to make up his mind about the arboretum and by 1889 had vetoed two proposals, leaving Olmsted at a loss to know what to suggest next. Then, in 1890, he had a serious clash with Stanford's manager, Ariel Lathrop, over control of the construction. Lathrop had suddenly dismissed the local engineer that Olmsted had placed in charge of the field work four years before. After Stanford supported Lathrop in the dismissal, Olmsted received no further reports or requests for advice and, after a time, resigned from the entire project.[26]

That he bore Leland Stanford no ill will at the end of their association is attested by the fact that, on reading about the opening of the university in 1891, he wrote a note of hearty congratulations to Stanford and his wife.[27] By that time a major portion of the plan for the main college complex had been carried out, and a strong expectation existed that the plan would continue to be followed. In the intervening years, however, the projected pattern for future expansion submitted by Olmsted and Coolidge has been badly neglected because of limited budgets and changing academic needs. The campus remains handsome, nevertheless, and though different in many ways from what its original designers envisioned, it retains the sense of unpretentious dignity toward which they aspired.[28] Ample proof of its success can be found in the many school and college buildings it has influenced, particularly in the state of California.

Chapter Six

Conservation: State and National Parks

The Mariposa Big Tree Grove and Yosemite Valley

Olmsted spent much of his career creating pastoral scenes in urban settings. For this work he used the materials provided by nature, re-making them to his own specifications. Yet he was equally sensitive to the monumental beauty of the untamed American landscape. He saw no need to refashion the Yosemite wilderness or Niagara Falls as he had refashioned the grounds of Central Park, for example. In-stead, the problem was to preserve these natural wonders from the depradations of civilization that had already begun to affect the eastern United States during the first half of the nineteenth century.

His first great opportunity came quite by accident after he as-sumed the superintendency of the Mariposa Mining Estate in Cali-fornia in 1863. In November of that year he ventured for the first time, by pack train, into the Sierras and saw the Mariposa Big Tree Grove, consisting of immense, ancient sequoias, each standing dis-tinct in the surrounding dense forest. He was instantly captivated by these trees, noting not only the extraordinary size of their trunks but their remarkably elegant cinnamon color. They seemed like "distinguished strangers [who] have come down to us from another world," he wrote to his wife, who was still in the East. One or two annual trips into the Big Tree Grove are the "highest gratifications peculiar to the country that you have to look forward to."[1]

In the summer of the following year, accompanied by a large party including his family, Olmsted undertook an extensive camping expedition into the region of the Mariposa Big Trees and then on to the fabulous Yosemite Valley for the first time. Nothing that he had read or heard had adequately prepared him for the awesomeness of this experience. Cascades threaded down great white granite cliffs almost a mile high, with the vast Sierras in the background. He thought he was seeing a glorious vision, a scenic allegory too wonderful to be believed. And it was the scene as a whole that most enthralled him: "The union of deepest sublimity with the deepest beauty of nature, not in one feature or another, not in one part or one scene or another, not in any landscape that can be framed by itself, but all around and wherever the visitor goes, constitutes the Yosemite the greatest glory of nature."[2]

Olmsted was especially gratified to realize that the unique beauty of this valley had recently been recognized officially by the United States government. The previous March, in the midst of the Civil War, Senator John Conness of California had introduced a bill in Congress, granting the Mariposa Big Tree Grove and Yosemite Valley, then part of the public domain, to the state of California on the condition that the area should be held "for public use, resort and recreation and shall be held inalienable for all time." The bill was subsequently passed in June 1864, and President Lincoln, performing an act not much noticed at the time, signed it into law.[3]

The United States national parks were born at that moment although Yosemite was not yet national, but state-owned: it was not to come under federal control as a park for some years. At the time, no tradition of great scenic parks existed anywhere in the world: to protect an area and conserve it for recreational enjoyment was a policy that had never before been adopted for the management of land from the public domain. Surprisingly, there was no strong organized public movement in favor of such parks, and Congress did not seem to have any special interest in the idea, despite the fact that the Yosemite Valley was already a renowned scenic marvel attracting hundreds of visitors annually, some from great distances.

Undoubtedly, the spirit of nineteenth-century romantic idealism played a part in spawning the proposal to preserve a scenic place like Yosemite. Joined to this spirit of idealism was certainly a practical concern to protect America's great natural resources. A third factor was probably the national desire to measure up to European civilization. The realization was dawning that the dazzling attractions of the American landscape could be compared favorably to those of the Swiss Alps, for example. Thus, although America might still be inferior to Europe in the arts, the awesome scenery of the mountainous West gave the nation something with which it could at last compete with Europe on an equal footing.[4]

The claim has sometimes been made that Olmsted was the theorist behind the creation of Yosemite National Park, but no evidence exists to suggest any theory at all preceding its establishment. There is little definite knowledge concerning the Conness bill. Conness said that the idea had been presented to him by some constituents, whom he described only as gentlemen "of fortune, of taste and of refinement." A letter to Conness from Israel Ward Raymond, California representative of the Central American Steamship Transit Company, has been preserved in which Raymond recommended the reservation of Yosemite. Olmsted may or may not have supported Raymond's suggestion.[5]

Preliminary Report on Yosemite

In the fall of 1864, Governor Frederick F. Low of California named Olmsted as a member of the first board of commissioners to have authority over the Yosemite Valley and the adjoining Big Tree Grove. The board consisted of eight members, including Olmsted, Israel Ward Raymond, Josiah Dwight Whitney, director of the California State Geological Survey, and William Ashburner, with whom Olmsted had become acquainted in San Francisco and with whom he had shared his family expedition to Yosemite. By agreement among themselves, Olmsted became chairman of the group. By stipulation of the governor, all propositions for the improvement of the land grant were to be reviewed by Olmsted. With his instinctive grasp of what was important and his talent for acting quickly, he had the territory surveyed and mapped in order that roads to and through it could be planned according to his detailed instructions. He advanced five hundred dollars out of his own pocket for the survey because the state had not yet made appropriations to cover this expense.[6]

The writing of a preliminary report on the future management of Yosemite as a public preserve logically fell to Olmsted. This task gave him another opportunity to construct a philosophy of land use for the public good. In August 1865, he invited the other commissioners to come into the Yosemite Valley for a meeting, which was attended also by some distinguished visitors, among them Schuyler Colfax, speaker of the United States House of Representatives; Samuel Bowles, editor of the *Springfield* (Massachusetts) *Republican*; Albert D. Richardson of the *New York Tribune*; William Bross, lieutenant governor of Illinois; and Charles Allen, attorney general of Massachusetts.[7] In his landmark report, delivered around a campfire to the assembled group, Olmsted enunciated what he considered the philosophical principles underlying the establishment of state and national parks—the fundamental purposes, social values, and appropriate development of great scenic areas, some of which he had never imagined even existed until he came west.

In his report on Yosemite, as earlier in his writings on Central Park, Olmsted demonstrated the qualities of a conservative social reformer with a distinctive theory about the role that public parks ought to play in a democratic society. "The Yosemite Valley and the Mariposa Big Tree Grove" was the first systematic exposition in America of the individual's right to enjoy large, impressive public reservations of natural scenery and, also, the government's obligation to protect him in the exercise of that right. For Olmsted, using language sometimes intentionally evocative of Thomas Jefferson, one aspect of the individual's pursuit of happiness, providing both physical and moral refreshment, was the contemplation of such scenery.

Fragmentary suggestions of Olmsted's theory, which has since his time become a fundamental policy of the National Park Service, had appeared in the writings of earlier Americans. Jefferson himself, refusing to sell land around the Natural Bridge in Virginia in 1815, had written: "I view it in some degree as a public trust and would on no consideration permit the bridge to be injured, defaced or masked from the public view."[8] And in 1833, George Catlin, a painter and explorer who had traveled up the Missouri River into Indian country, proposed that certain western regions might in the future be preserved "in their pristine beauty and wildness" as national parks.[9] As the nineteenth century progressed, writers like Irving, Cooper, Bryant, and Thoreau and landscape painters like Thomas Cole, Albert Bierstadt, and Frederic Church were educating Americans to appreciate the beauties of natural scenery at the same time that the demand for rural public parks in cities was growing stronger.

Although Olmsted in his Yosemite report emphasized the rights of the people in a democratic society to enjoy great scenic areas, he rejected the idea, now all too prevalent, that parks should facilitate access for the greatest number of people who can be accommodated and should provide whatever activities the popular sentiments of the time seem to favor. Instead, he insisted that the justification for the use of the parks must be found in the long-term judgment of the people, always guided by trained and enlightened leadership. He believed that this leadership should be responsible for the recreation of all citizens but had a special obligation to the great mass of people that do not have available the opportunities enjoyed by the rich. Those few who are rich enough, he argued, reserve for themselves rural retreats as large and luxurious as those of the European aristocracy. They take the choicest natural scenes and the most favored grounds devoted to recreation. And unless the government intervenes to stop this practice, "all places favorable in scenery to the recreation of the mind and body will be closed against the great body of the people."[10]

Olmsted went on to observe that the reason the governing classes of Europe had frequently assumed control of the great scenic resources was not simply out of selfishness but because they were convinced that the masses were incapable of cultivating a true enjoyment of beauty in either nature or art. This class distinction he found both false and repugnant. He utterly rejected any policy that treated ordinary people as passive objects to be entertained at only the most superficial level.[11]

Of paramount importance to Olmsted was the preservation of the natural scenery in as pristine a state as possible. These mountains and forests had been formed over millions of years without man's intervention. Therefore, all artificial constructions inharmonious with the scenery should be prohibited. He realized that it was common practice in his age for men to take from the land whatever material profit they could—whether timber, game, ore, or crops. He insisted, however, that it was the duty of the commissioners to draw up regulations preventing a wanton or careless disregard, by anyone entering Yosemite or the Big Tree Grove, of the rights of posterity as well as those of contemporary visitors. To make the grant readily accessible, he also urged that a few roads and bridges be constructed, as inconspicuously as possible, leading into Yosemite, circling the valley, and connecting it to the Mariposa Grove. The roads would serve as protection against forest fires that might otherwise endanger the magnificent trees.[12]

Olmsted's Report Suppressed

Olmsted did not stay on in California more than a couple of months after presenting his Yosemite report. Yielding to the pleas of Calvert Vaux, he decided to return east to resume his career as a landscape architect. He could not have foreseen that several problems with the grant of the public lands to California would block prompt action to establish a permanent Yosemite State Reservation based on his recommendations. The grant provided no federal funds with which to reimburse those who would have to give up property within the area. As a result, years of litigation over these holdings limited public access to them. In addition, two of the commissioners appointed by Governor Low had divided loyalties. Josiah Whitney and William Ashburner, leading members of the California State Geological Survey, feared that the state legislature might grant funds for Yosemite at the expense of the Geological Survey, which had to battle continually for funds to carry on its scientific work. Whitney tried to prevent the legislature from contributing to the College of California, and the existing evidence suggests that he and Ashburner, taking advantage of their position as commissioners, quietly suppressed Olmsted's report, which they knew included a request for $37,000. The fact is that the document never even reached the floor of the legislature.[13]

After his return to New York City, Olmsted heard this story of intrigue through private correspondence from California. Rather than involve Whitney and Ashburner in a public quarrel in this instance, however, he chose to let the alleged injustice pass and paid no public attention to it. Governor Low officially acknowledged his resignation from the Yosemite Commission in 1867.[14] It is ironic that most of Olmsted's report of 1865, now generally recognized as one of the most significant historical documents of what became the state and national park movement, disappeared for many years, leaving only a few provocative traces. An imperfect copy was finally discovered in the Olmsted office in Brookline in 1952 and was then reconstructed and published by Laura Wood Roper in that year.[15]

The California state legislature, which never saw Olmsted's report, approved only a meager $12,000 appropriation for the Yosemite Commission. But more importantly, the legislators were unable on their own to formulate a sound and comprehensive policy for administering the reservation. If Olmsted's report had been available to them, they might have been able to protect the Yosemite Valley from the private exploitation that jeopardized it in the next few decades. As it was, the state found the responsibility of maintaining the property increasingly onerous and allowed it to fall into neglect. As a result, naturalist John Muir launched a relentless campaign to save Yosemite from logging, grazing, and many other kinds of misuse.[16]

Olmsted worked, frequently behind the scenes, to obtain signatures from influential friends for a petition to Congress on behalf of the sanctity of Yosemite. In 1890, he wrote a pamphlet, "Governmental Preservation of National Scenery," in which he protested vigorously the imminent cutting of young trees in the region and charged the current commissioners with a "narrow, short-sighted and market-place view of the duty of the State in the premises."[17] Finally, in 1906, California ceded the park lands back to the federal government, and Congress turned the area into Yosemite National Park, as it is known today.[18]

Preserving Niagara Falls

Olmsted's second great opportunity to champion the cause of conservation came with the campaign to save the natural scenery around Niagara Falls from the commercialization and blight into which it had fallen. When he delivered his report on Yosemite in 1865, one of his enthusiastic listeners was Samuel Bowles, with whom he subsequently struck up a friendship. Bowles was so stimulated by Olmsted's ideas that, in an account of his travels that he published after his return to New England, he proposed that reservations on the same plan as Yosemite and the Mariposa Big Trees be established throughout the nation at such places as Niagara Falls and the Adirondacks.[19]

During the nineteenth century Niagara Falls had developed into the most popular tourist attraction in the United States. But as speculators bought up the land around the falls, they leveled large areas for the construction of mills along the water's edge. In the process, many magnificent trees were destroyed, and claptrap buildings, shops, and refuse dumps appeared. At the same time, swarms of peddlers and petty swindlers infiltrated the region. Tourists were constantly being harassed and, by the 1860s, prevented from viewing the falls from any point on the American side without first paying an entry fee to some local landowner.[20] Frederic Church, whose huge painting entitled "Niagara Falls" captivated countless viewers after it was unveiled in 1857, warned of the rapidly approaching ruin of the scenery.

Olmsted had visited the falls from time to time ever since he was a six-year-old boy. In 1869, while working on the Buffalo park project, he invited his friends William Dorsheimer and H. H. Richardson to meet him at Niagara Falls village to discuss what might be done to combat the desecration.[21] Olmsted was concerned about the total physical environment of the falls, including the special conditions producing the unique wild growth on Goat Island, which separates the flow of the Niagara River into two cataracts, the American Falls and the Horseshoe Falls. "All these distinctive qualities, the great variety of the indigenous perennials and annuals, the rare beauty of the old woods, and the exceeding loveliness of the rock foliage" on Goat Island, he believed to be "a direct effect of the Falls, and as much a part of its majesty as the mist-cloud and the rainbow."[22]

No tangible progress occurred, however, until ten years later, in 1879, when Governor Lucius Robinson of New York appointed a commission to devise, in collaboration with representatives of the government of Ontario, a plan to establish a reservation around Niagara Falls. Olmsted became largely responsible for organizing and directing the long and arduous campaign. He was first involved in a complete survey of the American side authorized by the New York State legislature. Associated with him in this project was James T. Gardiner, director of the New York State Survey, who had previously helped survey and map the proposed Yosemite site for him in 1865.[23]

After having completed their task, Olmsted and Gardiner met with the New York and Ontario commissioners at Niagara Falls. Olmsted presented the general outlines of a plan to restore and preserve the natural beauty of the scenery. He proposed creating not a true park around Niagara but only a reservation including the islands above the falls and a strip on both sides of the Niagara River, wide enough for plantings to screen out the buildings behind them. Unnecessary landscape gardening and formal ornamentation were to be avoided. All of the commissioners present approved Olmsted's proposal, though in recommending it, the prime minister of Ontario urged that the governments of the United States and Canada should be considered the real principals in the arrangements. After all, he argued, the preservation of the falls should be a national responsibility since the Niagara River is an international boundary.[24]

Olmsted realized that, to get his proposal approved by the New York State legislature, the obstacle of powerfully entrenched private interests, such as manufacturers who considered Niagara Falls an exploitable resource, would have to be overcome. Thus, to influence the governor and legislature of New York, he enlisted the help of Dorsheimer, Church, and Charles Eliot Norton in preparing a petition containing the signatures of some of the most distinguished members of the Anglo-American community who supported the preservation of Niagara. When Olmsted's finished report appeared in 1880, about seven hundred people had signed it—probably as dazzling a list of notables as any such document has ever had. It even included all the justices of the United States Supreme Court.[25]

But even this endorsement by an international élite failed to impress Alonzo B. Cornell, the new governor of New York, who looked at the proposal only in terms of its cost to his state. Olmsted saw that a more systematic campaign would be necessary to publicize both the dangers to Niagara Falls and the value of his plan. In his long report on Yosemite fifteen years before, he had already established the rationale for setting aside areas of extraordinary scenic beauty in the public interest. That document had had no real impact, however, because of its suppression, so he had to restate the basic argument, and to keep repeating it with special reference to Niagara.[26]

To cultivate widespread public interest, Olmsted and Norton sponsored the preparation of many newspaper and magazine articles about Niagara. Two articulate young men whom they employed to go to the falls and write material for Buffalo, New York City, and Boston papers were Henry Norman, an Englishman recently graduated with honors from Harvard, and Jonathan Baxter Harrison, a Unitarian minister who had become a journalist. By 1882, however, it seemed clear that it would be impossible to coordinate the efforts of New York State with those of Ontario. A group of men active in the movement to preserve the falls, including Olmsted and Norton, decided at this point to give up the idea of establishing an international reservation. They recommended that New York act unilaterally to buy the land on its side of the Niagara River for a state reservation only. At Olmsted's request, a meeting was called early in 1883 in New York City at which the Niagara Falls Association was formed. Harrison, named secretary, was put in charge of flooding New York State with letters, pamphlets, and petitions.

At last, responding to aroused public opinion largely influenced by the steady barrage of educational propaganda, both the Assembly and the Senate of New York State passed the Niagara bill in 1883. By this time, Grover Cleveland had become governor, and one of his chief advisers was William Dorsheimer. Cleveland was quickly persuaded to sign the bill, and he appointed a Niagara commission of which Dorsheimer became president.[27]

Olmsted's Crucial Role

The struggle was not yet over. The appropriation bill for the bond issue to finance the purchase of land surrounding the falls subsequently ran into difficulty in the state legislature, and the Niagara Falls Association was once again mobilized to save it. Two years elapsed before the bill was finally passed by both houses of the legislature.[28] The new Niagara grounds were officially opened to the public in July 1885. Olmsted's role in the ultimately successful campaign had been crucial. Ten years later, his colleague Jonathan Baxter Harrison gave this assessment: "Success was obtained by the co-operation of multitudes; but the indispensable factor was Mr. Frederick Law Olmsted's thought. He was the real source, as he was the true director, of the movement, and but for him, there would be no State Reservation at Niagara today."[29] In perhaps no other enterprise of his long career did Olmsted reveal himself so clearly as the idealist who could convert his ideals into effective political action.

But Olmsted's involvement in the preservation of Niagara Falls continued. In 1886, the commissioners turned to Olmsted and Vaux to prepare a long-range plan for landscaping the state reservation, with special emphasis on Goat Island. Because of his long-standing conflict with Olmsted, Andrew Haswell Green, one of the commissioners appointed by Governor Cleveland, had wished to employ Vaux alone. The other commissioners disagreed, however, and the two men were consulted as a team once more.[30] In their report presented the following year, they considered the problem of designing a reservation that would accommodate large numbers of visitors to the falls without depriving them of the kind of experience for which the area had been created. They enunciated the following principle: "Nothing of an artificial character should be allowed a place on the property, no matter how valuable it might be under other circumstances and no matter at how little cost it may be had, the presence of which can be avoided consistently with the provision of necessary conditions for making the enjoyment of the natural scenery available."[31]

This was the same basic principle that Olmsted had followed in all of his public park work and that he had espoused in his Yosemite report as well. In their plan for Niagara Falls, he and Vaux acknowledged that such artificial constructions as shelters, picnic facilities, and walkways would be needed, as well as the restoration of eroded areas. But they were opposed to any attempt at fancy landscaping, as they had consistently been in Central and Prospect parks, because they felt it would tend to distract visitors from the natural scenery. They were equally opposed to such developmental proposals as a handsome restaurant to be located on Goat Island just above the falls, since they argued that a short drive would give visitors easy access to hotels and restaurants outside the boundaries of the reservation.

Olmsted and Vaux also objected to a proposal that would have allowed visitors to view Niagara Falls without ever leaving their carriages. In the first place, they observed very practically that each carriage would take up much more space than a pedestrian. Since as many as ten thousand people a day visited the falls even in the 1880s, they argued for the exclusion of carriages on the grounds of efficiency. But their real objection to carriages in the reservation was based on what had developed, especially for Olmsted, into a philosophy of leisure. One could simply not appreciate the beauties of Niagara Falls fully enough from a carriage. One had to take the time to see them at length and at leisure, experiencing them as a kind of overwhelming scenic presence. Thus to design the viewing areas to accommodate large numbers of carriages would introduce an artificial, urban experience clearly in conflict with the natural experience for which the reservation was intended.[32]

Olmsted demonstrated this principle in action one year when he and his wife vacationed at Niagara Falls with the Richardsons. After they arrived, Olmsted drove Richardson around leisurely for several hours before letting his friend and collaborator get even a glimpse of the falls. It was not until the next day that the two men, approaching Niagara quietly and gradually, took in the full view. By that time, Olmsted noted, Richardson had "caught the idea of throwing curiosity aside and avoiding amazement, and was willing to sit for hours in one place contemplatively enjoying the beauty, saying little of what was before us . . . but taking quiet pleasure and laying up pleasure."[33] It was this philosophy of leisure that Olmsted wanted to promote. Thus he insisted that the Niagara reservation be managed to encourage visitors to view the falls in the absorbed and contemplative way he had taught Richardson. A few years later he expressed essentially the same idea in his pamphlet about Yosemite as he remembered it on the eve of his departure for the East in 1865: "I felt the charm of the Yosemite much more at the end of a week than at the end of a day, much more after six weeks when the cascades were nearly dry, than after one week, and when, after having been in it, off and on, several months, I was going out, I said, 'I have not yet half taken it in.' "[34]

Olmsted's philosophy of leisure reflected his democratic belief in the capacity of even the ordinary working man to appreciate the experience of quiet solitude in a setting of unspoiled natural scenery. And the history of the state and national parks, as well as of reservations like Niagara, has proved him right. Niagara has remained a popular tourist attraction, and with every passing decade, the parks have drawn increasing numbers of visitors from a broad spectrum of society. Olmsted was also right in recognizing the importance of imaginative leadership in a democracy to safeguard the rights of the people and to provide opportunities for constructive recreation and leisure. This type of leadership has not always been forthcoming. Both Niagara and Yosemite have fallen victim to commercial blight in recent years. Niagara has always had its problems, but Yosemite has, particularly since the 1960s, suffered from periodic invasions of automobiles and overcrowded campgrounds. Drastic action, including limiting the number of visitors admitted at any given time, will be necessary to restore the natural serenity of the park.

Chapter Seven

The Heights: Biltmore and the World's Columbian Exposition of 1893

Planning Biltmore

The last years of Olmsted's professional practice offered him his two most spectacular opportunities in landscape architecture. In 1888, George Washington Vanderbilt, grandson of the commodore, asked him for guidance in the planning and design of Biltmore, a vast tract in the Great Smokies near Asheville, North Carolina, that would become the most lavish example of architectural opulence of its kind ever achieved in the United States. Then, in 1890, Olmsted was invited to recommend and plan a site for the World's Columbian Exposition of 1893, frequently called the Chicago World's Fair, which was to mark a high point of achievement in the arts of the United States.

Olmsted's relationship with the wealthy and powerful Vanderbilt family was well established. They had been neighbors on Staten Island, and he had already done work for George Vanderbilt's summer home at Bar Harbor, Maine, and for the site of the Vanderbilt family mausoleum on Staten Island before he was called upon to go down to Asheville and advise this twenty-six-year-old bachelor what to do with the land he was purchasing. George Vanderbilt had begun acquiring land after a trip to Asheville with his mother. On repeated visits to the small town, which was already becoming a resort for prosperous Northerners, he found it a pleasant refuge from northern winters and enjoyed riding horseback through the rolling, wooded countryside. On one excursion he found a spot that opened on the finest view he had seen in the region, with the French Broad River in the foreground and with a long view northwest toward Pisgah, the highest elevation in this range of the Blue Ridge Mountains. While other members of his family were erecting mansions on New York's fashionable Fifth Avenue, he decided he would like to have a house on this spot.

Vanderbilt had a vague idea, based on what he thought English country squires did with their property, of turning the two thousand acres he had so far accumulated into some sort of park. This was the point at which he engaged Olmsted to examine the property and tell him whether he had done anything "very foolish." Olmsted assured him that, if he had selected it for the invigorating air and splendid outlook, no mistake had been made. But Olmsted thought the acreage was unsuitable for a park. The soil seemed poor, the woods had been continually culled until only runts and saplings were left, and the topography was generally inappropriate for park scenery.

What Olmsted suggested instead was that the land be turned into a forest, partly as a hunting preserve for game but mainly as a project in forestry. Such a project would be profitable commercially and would also be of great value to the country as a "well organized and systematically conducted attempt in forestry, made on a large scale." He advised Vanderbilt to create a small park and gardens that would be visible from the house. Then, in keeping with the idea of a working estate, modeled on the European concept, a truck farm could be established along the river bottom lands nearby for fresh produce and a dairy farm established for milk and also for manure. Finally, the rest of the property could be made a forest through improving the existing woods and planting the old fields.[1] Vanderbilt was favorably impressed with this advice and decided to adopt it, placing Olmsted in charge of the overall plan.

Forestry had been practiced in England and Europe for centuries. In the Old World it had long been necessary to manage forests economically to provide a steady crop of timber and also to preserve a healthy and attractive growth of trees. In the New World, however, forestry yet scarcely existed. Since American forests seemed inexhaustible, there was little incentive to conserve and replenish them. Lumbermen were used to cutting recklessly and then abandoning deforested areas to move on to newly discovered virgin growth. The idea that a forest could yield good timber and still be an organic, enduring entity was still a novelty.

Olmsted had long been concerned about the depletion of American forests. On several occasions he had called attention in the *Nation* to the relationship between forests and water supply. He had worked with Charles Sprague Sargent, the nation's foremost authority on trees, to establish the Arnold Arboretum in Boston and to launch *Garden and Forest*, a weekly magazine treating landscape architecture, forestry, and horticulture. The two men had also joined in a search for ways to protect both West Coast redwood and Adirondack forests from the ravages of lumbermen and fires. And Olmsted's proposal for Stanford University had provided for reforesting the nearby hills and setting up an arboretum.[2]

Collaborating with Richard Morris Hunt

George Vanderbilt at first intended to build a large frame house on his property. But after a tour of the French chateau country along the Loire Valley, he was persuaded by his architect, Richard Morris Hunt, to build instead an extravagant mansion characteristic of the large country estates that fascinated the wealthy in this era.[3] Hunt, the first American architect to return from the Ecole Nationale des Beaux Arts in Paris, was enormously popular with wealthy industrialists and financial tycoons who wanted magnificent houses to confirm their new position in American society. He was a dedicated Francophile, and his clients in this age of the fabled rise of great American fortunes believed that nothing could better display their status than apparent familiarity with things European.

Whatever doubts Olmsted might privately have had about the idea of an aristocratic French Renaissance chateau set down in a wild, mountainous region of rural America, he realized that the picturesque style he had frequently championed had a formidable rival in the new interest in a formal architecture and landscape. Richardson's Romanesque style for public buildings and his informal, wooden shingle style for houses, which Olmsted had found congenial to his own natural approach to the landscape, were being abandoned by the 1880s in favor of a classical style, and the leader of the new architectural generation was unquestionably Richard Morris Hunt.[4]

Olmsted had already worked with Hunt in the siting and design of the Vanderbilt mausoleum on Staten Island. These two opinionated men had differed publicly in the architectural dispute about the New York State capitol at Albany, and Hunt had lost out in the heated struggle against Olmsted, Richardson, and Eidlitz over whether the design should be Renaissance or Romanesque. Olmsted sensed that he would have problems in collaborating with Hunt on the Biltmore project, but the two men had respect for each other's talents and managed, as things turned out, to work together reasonably well. Hunt did the actual design of the chateau, built of limestone transported six hundred miles from Indiana, but Olmsted provided the detailed instructions on how it should be placed in relation to the lay of the land and the splendid outlook.

Olmsted recognized at once that the architectural style of the chateau would require a different treatment of landscape from that of the public parks he had created: a picturesque setting would be completely inappropriate. Thus he developed the immediate grounds as an extension of the classical, geometric lines of the mansion. The result was that, however eccentric and possibly unjustified the French appearance might be, the house and grounds were built simultaneously and have the integrity of a single architectonic composition. It was Olmsted's decision that a great terrace should be added on the southeast side, protected by walls from the blustery northwest winds and providing below it a sheltered ramble for outdoor exercise in inclement weather. Also on the east, he designed a broad, formal esplanade with a long vista much like the great allée at Vaux-le-Vicomte near Paris. Double rows of trees bordered the sides of the esplanade, and in the central panel of turf was a reflecting pool.[5]

In planning the main approach to the house, Olmsted worked hard to achieve a breathtaking effect. He wanted the impact of a carefully orchestrated visual experience and designed a beautiful, winding drive in the picturesque style that would deliberately sequester the visitor for a time among the ravines and pools of a deep natural forest. No distant views or open spaces would break the seclusion "until the visitor passed with an abrupt transition into the enclosure of the trim, level, open, airy, spacious, thoroughly artificial Court, and the Residence, with its orderly dependencies, breaks suddenly and fully upon him."[6] Elsewhere on the estate he designed a road system that created handsome vistas, using the natural topography to develop curving pleasure drives and unexpected approaches.

The landscape architecture around Biltmore was planned so that, as the visitor strolled away from the house, the grounds would become less formal and he could move gradually from civility to the relatively wild. Here Olmsted used his knowledge of country house settings, placing a large conservatory to the south of the entire house-complex, at the foot of the descending terraces of the formal gardens.[7] Beyond these features, and already far enough away from the chateau to give a feeling of wild nature, he located what he named the Vernal Garden, now maintained as an experimental ground for azaleas.[8] Thus he was able to provide an unobtrusive blend of the classical and the pastoral after all. Though the grounds immediately around the mansion were essentially formal, the windows facing west looked out upon an English deer park that stretched down to the banks of the French Broad River.

Forest Management at Biltmore

But for Olmsted, the most absorbing work at Biltmore lay in the thousands of acres of farmland and forest that Vanderbilt was continually buying up. Although many of the fields had been overrun by scrub pine, Olmsted saw that they could be made to sustain a

wide variety of trees and shrubs. Furthermore, he was able to persuade Vanderbilt that, even before the forest became profitable,
overseeing such a project would be an occupation "far more interesting to a man of poetic temperament than any of those commonly
considered appropriate to a country-seat life." But it was characteristic of Olmsted that he regarded the forestry project from the beginning as semipublic in potential. Thus, part of his enthusiasm
was in the fact that Vanderbilt would have, besides the immediate
enjoyment, the satisfaction of knowing that he was doing his
country an "inestimable service" by financing its first large-scale
forestry experiment.[9] Here was another thread that had run throughout Olmsted's career from his early days of scientific farming at
Sachem's Head and on Staten Island. Scientific planning was in-

Biltmore: Photograph of the Italian Garden with its pools, located
below the south side of the Esplanade at Biltmore, Asheville, North
Carolina. A corner of the chateau is visible at the upper right.
(Courtesy of Olmsted Associates, Inc., and the Frances Loeb Library, Harvard Graduate School of Design)

extricably linked for him with social planning, and he continued until his retirement to focus his professional intelligence in a variety of ways on social betterment.

As work on the vast expanses of field and forest continued over a period of several years, one section after another, Olmsted clearly enjoyed solving the landscape problems he confronted in their own terms, free now from the necessity of making the design "look French."[10] He also enjoyed working with George Vanderbilt, with whom he was on easy personal terms. Until he retired in 1895, Olmsted went to Biltmore two or three times a year, and he often stayed for weeks at a time. On occasion he traveled with Vanderbilt in the millionaire's private railway car. During construction Vanderbilt and his guests, including Olmsted and Hunt and their associates, stayed in what was called the Brick House, one of the more substantial buildings on the premises. There Olmsted indulged in evenings of whist and other diversions after long hours spent in the saddle personally overseeing the elaborate designs he was creating in the backwoods of North Carolina.

The lavish scale of operations at Biltmore was legendary even in this Gilded Age. Perhaps the most impressive single feature was the private railway branch line built to transport construction materials from the main line to the house site. Nearly three miles long, it cost over $77,000 and was designed to be removed upon completion of the project. Olmsted took these matters in stride. His firm employed and directed the engineers under whose supervision the surveying, roadbuilding, construction of bridges and drains, and planting of trees and shrubs were done.[11] Then, too, he oversaw the development of the English-cottage style village of Biltmore, including houses for the staff of the estate, an office still used today, a railway station, shops, a factory for the manufacture of bricks, and a saw mill.

It was Olmsted's idea to start a nursery where many of the plants could be set for two or three years after having been gathered locally: they could be transplanted for much less than they could be bought commercially. As the nursery developed, Chauncey D. Beadle, a Cornell graduate whose botanical knowledge awed Olmsted, was put in charge of it, and toward the end of 1891, Olmsted selected Gifford Pinchot to head the forestry operations of the estate, which represented the first large-scale experiment in scientific forest management in the United States.[12]

Pinchot, who was later to become chief of the Division of Forestry in the Department of Agriculture in Washington, D.C., was exactly the right man for the job. A well-to-do New Yorker of French descent, he had decided upon graduation from Yale in 1889 to make a career of forestry even though this was a profession new to America. He furthered his education at the Ecole Nationale Forestière in France and made the acquaintance of the leading foresters of Europe, among them Sir Dietrich Brandis, who had introduced systematic forestry to Burma and India. After listening to Pinchot's dreams of bringing forestry to the United States, Brandis had replied: "Nothing general can be done until some State or large individual owner makes the experiment and proves for America what is so well established in Europe, that forest management will pay."[13]

George Vanderbilt provided the opportunity for which Pinchot had been waiting. On his return to the United States, Pinchot stopped at Asheville during a trip south and found Biltmore ideal for forest management on a large scale.[14] By then the estate, to which Vanderbilt continued to add, consisted of many thousands of acres. Forty thousand trees and shrubs were growing on forty acres of nursery. Hundreds of acres of fields were planted in white pine, and Olmsted's "Project of Operations for Improving the Forest of Biltmore" was well under way. Olmsted invited Pinchot to Biltmore in October, 1891, and interviewed him again the next month in Brookline. After Pinchot was finally appointed forester to the Biltmore Estate two months later, Olmsted gave him considerable freedom to exercise his competence. Pinchot declared later that Olmsted had "one of the best minds I have ever had the good luck to encounter." He appreciated, too, the fact that Olmsted took the profession of forestry seriously.[15]

Olmsted and Gifford Pinchot, working together with the support of George Vanderbilt, created not only Biltmore Forest, on land surrounding the house, but Pisgah Forest, the great area of semi-wilderness that became the Pisgah National Forest. From the beginning of his association with Pinchot, Olmsted discussed the idea of inaugurating a national school of forestry at Biltmore. But not until after his retirement, and after Pinchot's resignation of his post as forester, was such a school finally established. The Biltmore School of Forestry served for some twenty years as a badly needed training ground for professional foresters.[16]

Planning a Scientific Arboretum

Another project that Olmsted envisioned for Biltmore was an arboretum. Since his plans for one at Stanford had never materialized, he had a special interest in laying one out at Biltmore to border roads that would be built from the chateau to the next valley south. Included were to be an experiment station and dendrological museum of wide scientific interest. But problems with the arboretum soon developed, as problems had previously arisen at Stanford. Olmsted had set his heart on a thoroughly scientific arboretum and wanted Vanderbilt to employ a highly trained botanist to compile a careful planting list and to act as curator. Vanderbilt, however, had no great interest in this kind of scientific arboretum. What he wanted was mainly a pleasure ground of a more popular and ornamental character. This conflict was never resolved to Olmsted's satisfaction, and eventually, after his retirement, the project dwindled. After the turn of the century, when Vanderbilt overextended himself financially, the arboretum became an early casualty.[17]

During the last few years of his life, Olmsted felt for Biltmore what he had felt for Central Park at the beginning of his career. It came to absorb more and more of his attention, and he frequently thought of it as though it were his own estate. He sensed that it would be one of his last major works, and he was also preoccupied with the importance of Biltmore as his greatest achievement in the landscaping of private homes and estates. His firm was preeminent in public park design, but it had had no other crowning successes in private work. All the more reason, he felt, to concentrate at the end on "the most distinguished private place, not only of America, but of the world, forming at this *period*."[18]

It is a sad commentary on the current state of Olmsted's creations that, of all his major works, Biltmore is the one now being maintained most nearly in the spirit of the original. After Vanderbilt's death in 1914, his widow deeded a considerable portion of forest holdings to the federal government, and Pisgah National Forest, the first national forest in the United States, had a nucleus upon which to grow. In the 1930s, the remainder of Biltmore was converted from a personal property of the Vanderbilt heirs into a private corporation, and the house and grounds were opened to the public. They seem more appropriate as a tourist museum and showplace of international importance than they ever did as the residence and grounds of a small family. Today the house, sited as Olmsted planned, is surrounded by the original twelve thousand acres of the estate, which is still useful to the local community as a demonstration center for modern dairy farming and sustained yield forestry.[19]

The World's Columbian Exposition of 1893

In 1890, as the four-hundredth anniversary of Columbus's discovery of America approached, Olmsted was invited to Chicago to examine possible locations for a world's fair to be held there. Chicago had been designated that year by Congress as host for what had been named the World's Columbian Exposition, to be opened to the public in May 1893. Although the opening should more appropriately have occurred in 1892, the date was pushed back a year to allow greater time for preparation. The Chicago fair was heralded as the sixth great international conclave to be sponsored during the second half of the nineteenth century, primarily in order to promote the exchange of the most advanced products of the industrial revolution. In previous fairs, these products had been exhibited in huge halls of glass and iron made possible by new technology in casting metal. For the first exposition in 1851, organized by Prince Albert of England, Sir Joseph Paxton had designed the famed Crystal Palace in London. For the Exposition Universelle of 1889 in Paris, Gustave Eiffel had erected his soaring and audacious Eiffel Tower, a landmark in the use of structural steel.

Now at last, a major international exposition was to be held in the New World. Almost immediately a controversy arose regarding a site in Chicago. When the commissioners in charge could not agree on one, they consulted Olmsted, who arrived in August 1890, accompanied by his talented junior partner Henry Sargent Codman, whose experience at the 1889 exposition in Paris made him a valued associate. After examining seven possible sites, some on the shore of Lake Michigan and some inland, Olmsted and Codman decided that the three lakeshore locations had more to offer. Of the three, the northernmost seemed the most desirable but had to be eliminated because the local railroads were unwilling to extend their tracks to the site. The middle location was too cramped near the commercial center of Chicago, so the choice went to the southernmost location. Olmsted already knew this site—called Jackson Park—well because he and Vaux had made a plan for it in 1871, when the land was reserved by the city for park use.

Very little had been done toward creating the proposed chain of interconnecting lagoons on what was still a swampy, desolate piece of sandy soil with a few scrub oaks. Olmsted decided that his old design for a park was, with some adaptations, appropriate for a fairground as well. Previously he and Vaux had proposed dredging channels inward from Lake Michigan and depositing the resulting sandy sludge on the banks to give them greater height and variety. Now he amended the plan so that the lagoons would have the character of canals with strong vertical retaining walls in keeping with the numerous exhibition buildings for which they would provide terracelike bases. Excavated material could be used for filling in behind the channel walls, and the total effect would be somewhat similar to that of the canals of Venice.[20]

At this point Olmsted and Codman were ready to confer with the prominent architectural firm of Burnham and Root in Chicago.

Daniel H. Burnham, with a solid reputation as an efficient manager of major building projects, had been instrumental in securing the fair for the city. For most of its duration he was director of works and chairman of its consulting board, composed of the various architects, landscape architects, and engineers. John Wellborn Root, his younger partner, was a brilliant designer. From the start, the four men found themselves in general agreement about the selection of Jackson Park and its treatment. A genial spirit prevailed that was to characterize the monumental interprofessional collaboration of the whole enterprise. That same August, F. L. Olmsted and Company were officially appointed consulting landscape architects to the fair, and Burnham and Root were appointed consulting architects.[21]

But despite the four consultants' unanimous recommendation, the national World's Columbian Commission, composed of distinguished citizens selected by the president, expressed a decided preference for Washington Park, the inland park site connected to Jackson Park by a long, narrow strip of land. By 1890, the plan of Olmsted and Vaux for this park, done twenty years earlier, had been partially carried out. For this reason Washington Park seemed to the untrained eyes of the national commissioners more finished, whereas the Jackson Park area looked forbidding.[22] As a result, the four consultants hastened to draft a second report, in which they pointed out that Jackson Park offered original soil to be worked with and directly adjoined the "one distinguishing natural, historic, and poetic feature of this part of the American continent—its great inland seas."[23] They also suggested that Washington Park could be used as an overflow ground. The eloquence of their second report helped carry the day. Regarding the approval of the Jackson Park site, Olmsted afterward commented:

In the end the Commission accepted our advice, not, I think, because a majority of its members understood the grounds of it, but because they could not be led to believe that we should have given this advice without having, as experts, sound reasons for so doing. The result was due to respect for professional judgment. Comparing this experience with

some in my earlier professional life, I can but think it manifests an
advance in civilization.[24]

A Controlling Plan for the Exposition

Olmsted, Codman, Burnham, and Root next set to work on a
controlling plan for the exposition. The basic design was Olmsted's,
using from his 1871 plan a sight line approximately perpendicular
to the lakefront. Balanced on this line would be a great architectonic
space with buildings facing upon a large body of water, or basin, in
the center. This Court of Honor, as it was called, would serve as the
dignified and impressive entrance hall to the fair: all visitors arriving by train from the west or by boat from the east would pass
through it. From the central court, extending north at right angles,
a canal would lead out of the basin into a series of lagoons on which
other buildings would face. Thus all principal buildings would have
a water as well as a land approach.[25]

Near the middle of the lagoon system, a wooded island of about
fifteen acres already existed and, according to the designers' plan,
would be kept free of conspicuous buildings so that it could be
somewhat secluded and sylvan, a place of rest for visitors tired of the
bustle of the crowds. From information furnished them, the four
consultants determined the number and sizes of the buildings. Olmsted himself made a careful study of the expected circulation patterns of the fairgrounds to make sure there would be adequate and
convenient pedestrian links between the buildings. The borders of
the site were to be unified by a circumferential trolley system, and
the entire fair was linked to the railroad lines. Olmsted was far
ahead of his time in treating the various sections of the grounds as
what would today be termed a series of superblocks, with corridors
facilitating a free circulation of vehicles and pedestrians, in addition
to boat transportation on the lagoons.[26] Root and Codman roughed
out a large-scale drawing on brown paper, and the entire controlling
plan for the exposition was officially adopted by the national commissioners in December 1890.

As director of works, Daniel Burnham was authorized to select distinguished architects to design the main buildings. Among those he chose were Richard Morris Hunt of New York, with whom Olmsted was already working at Biltmore; McKim, Mead, and White of New York; Peabody and Stearns of Boston; Van Brunt and Howe of Kansas City; and Adler and Sullivan of Chicago. Augustus Saint-Gaudens, the leading sculptor of the day, was persuaded to advise on sculptural decoration and to help select artists to execute it. He enlisted the services of Daniel Chester French to create the colossal sixty-five-foot female figure of the Republic at one end of the Court of Honor, and of Frederick MacMonnies to contribute the grandiose Columbia fountain at the other end. The spirit of teamwork was extraordinary as each of the participants tried generously to add to the harmony of the whole rather than to glorify himself. Saint-Gaudens is reported to have remarked to Burnham, when all the architects and sculptors were assembled, "Look here, old fellow, do you realize that this is the greatest meeting of artists since the fifteenth century?"[27]

For over two years, work on the fair proceeded at a strenuous pace under Burnham's driving hand. Soon after its start he asked Francis D. Millet to coordinate the work of painters as Saint-Gaudens was doing for that of sculptors. Some of the most accomplished mural painters like Kenyon Cox and Edwin H. Blashfield took part. Since it had been decided that the exteriors of all the buildings of the central group would be uniformly white, Millet organized what Burnham called the "white-wash gang" to execute a new method for spraying on paint with squirt guns. The white paint created the effect of a mirage glittering on the shore of Lake Michigan and caused the fairgrounds to be known as the White City.

The only building designed as a permanent structure was the Art Gallery, copied from a Prix de Rome model for the Chicago Art Museum. All the rest were constructed of staff, an inexpensive mixture of plaster and fibrous binding material fitted on skeletons or armatures made of wood and chicken wire.[28] Planning for a temporary event was a new experience for Olmsted: in his parks he had become accustomed to looking years and even decades ahead for the full achievement of the effects he wanted. Still, he recognized

World's Columbian Exposition: Lagoons and gondolas were an integral part of the Court of Honor, the core of the Olmsted-Codman plan for the World's Columbian Exposition of 1893. The original pen-and-ink drawing is by Harry Fenn. (Courtesy of the Bland Collection, Prints Division, The New York Public Library, Astor, Lenox and Tilden Foundations)

precisely the nature of the job to be done. Broad landscaping effects would be out of place, and his own work would have to be accommodated to the requirements of the designated buildings, approximately 150 in number.

Despite the large number of buildings, Olmsted was determined to create a natural, unobtrusive look in the miles of shore plantings along the lagoons. He used aquatic plants profusely, rooting them partly below and partly above the surface of the water to give the lagoons the appearance of having been there for many years. He favored plants native to the Middle West but used a few mildly exotic ones to add richness to the general effect. Taking infinite pains to guard against the destruction of shore plantings by the movement of the shore ice during winter months, he proposed that this ice, when it formed, be cut free from the body of lake ice and held in place with stakes until it thawed in the spring.[29]

Olmsted devoted about half of his professional time to the fair, and even more after the untimely death of Henry Codman just four months before the official opening in 1893. Even such seemingly small details as the kinds of boats to be used were of concern to him. He insisted that their main purpose was not for convenient transportation but for decoration. His forceful letters to Burnham when he was away from Chicago reveal his conviction that small, graceful boats would be a valuable original feature of the exposition, greatly enhancing the festive atmosphere.[30] After a cruise on the Thames in an electric launch during a trip to England, he wrote his partners a detailed account of the kind of silent electric boats he wanted, specifying their exact seating arrangements, styles of awnings, and furnishings.[31] In addition to the fifty electric-powered launches he eventually obtained, he ordered gondolas that were built and equipped in Venice. And at his suggestion, full-sized replicas of Columbus's three ships were brought over from Spain.[32]

Olmsted was interested, also, in the use of waterfowl to lend animation to the lagoons, and he studied the effects of bridges in extending perspectives and in connecting terraces and buildings to create a sense of visual order.[33] Paying special attention to the wooded island in the midst of the lagoons, he fought a running battle to try to keep it free from displays and organized entertainments. It was in great demand for use in a variety of ways, and finally he was forced to allow a Japanese temple, along with certain horticultural exhibits, to be placed there. The results proved to be relatively unobtrusive, but he was not pleased with this alteration of his original intention.[34]

For the most part, main buildings of the fair were spectacular exercises in elaborate Beaux Arts classical design, influenced strongly by the eastern architects of the school of Richard Morris Hunt. A uniformity existed not only in the whiteness of the structures around the Court of Honor but in their sixty-foot cornice line, working toward a Beaux Arts magnificence that would be easily appreciated by both naive and sophisticated visitors. Hardly a column or pilaster was left undecorated: the labor alone was astonishing. Nothing failed to aim at grandeur, whether in the daytime reflections Olmsted created in the waterways or in the glamour of the electric lighting, then still a novelty, to outline the buildings at night.

In March 1893, shortly before the exposition opened, a gala banquet for some 200 guests was held in New York City to honor Daniel Burnham, the director of works, and to celebrate the occasion near at hand. Traveling in the South at the time, Olmsted was not present, but his contribution not only to the fair itself but to landscape architecture generally was eloquently recognized. Burnham, for whom the dinner was meant as a testimonial, took the opportunity to address the distinguished diners:

Each of you knows the name and genius of him who stands first in the heart and confidence of American artists, the creator of your own parks and many other city parks. He it is who has been our best adviser and our common mentor. In the highest sense he is the planner of the Exposition—Frederick Law Olmsted. No word of his has fallen to the ground among us since he first joined us some thirty months ago. As artist, he paints with lakes and wooded slopes; with lawns and banks and forest-covered hills; with mountainsides and ocean views. He should stand where I do tonight, not for his deeds of later years alone, but for what his brain has wrought and his pen has taught for half a century.[35]

At the same dinner, Charles Eliot Norton toasted the friend he had admired for many years:

The general design of the grounds and of the arrangement of the buildings was in every respect noble, original, and satisfactory, a work of a fine art not generally included in the list of poetic arts, but one of the most important of them all to America—that of the landscape architect. Of all American artists, Frederick Law Olmsted, who gave the design for the laying out of the grounds of the World's Fair, stands first in the production of great works which answer the needs and give expression to the life of our immense and miscellaneous democracy.[36]

Results of the Exposition

The exposition opened its gates to the public as scheduled on 1 May 1893. Olmsted was disappointed that the grounds were not completely ready in time, but even in the unfinished setting, the ceremonies were impressive. A crowd estimated at nearly half a million was packed around the Court of Honor to hear President Grover Cleveland's opening day address. Olmsted purposely stayed away from the dignitaries' platform in order to keep a watchful eye on the proceedings throughout the fairgrounds. Although he had to leave Chicago for the East several weeks later, he returned for a few days in June to observe the fair in full swing. Even after that, he continued to write recommendations to Burnham. Feeling, for instance, that the mood of the crowds tended to be too serious, he suggested that small parties of strolling banjo players, lemonade peddlers in picturesque dress, and musicians on the boats might be introduced to lighten it.[37] This sort of colorful pageantry appealed to him, as he also relished the idea of bringing together holiday crowds from all over the world.

The fair was designed to last only six months. After receiving hundreds of thousands of visitors, it closed and most of its buildings were torn down. But Olmsted had another design in view that

would be permanent. He was ultimately content to see these buildings of lath and plaster crumble, for then he would finally have the
park he had first conceived for Chicago years before. Part of the
genius of his plan for the fair was his anticipation of this transition
—and with minimal costs to the city of Chicago.

Despite the problems and uncertainties with which he had been
faced, Olmsted was satisfied on the whole with the results of the
fair. He had taken particular pleasure in the comradeship among
the planners and thought that a major accomplishment lay in the
demonstration of efficient cooperation among specialists in the arts
that was possible in a civilized society. For the first time in America,
sculpture and painting had been introduced on a grand scale as
integral parts of an architectural whole. The fair proved what
Olmsted had realized years before in his work with men like Vaux
and Richardson: that to be truly successful, a collaboration means
joint involvement from the beginning of a project in an open-
minded acceptance of mutual help.[38]

Perhaps the best known result of the Columbian Exposition was
the noticeable increase of public interest in civic design. The enthusiasm generated over the White City far exceeded anything its
creators had expected. William Dean Howells, preeminent man of
letters during the period, saw the fair through the eyes of Aristides
Homos in "Letters of an Altrurian Traveller": "I feel as if I had
caught a glimpse of the glorious capitals which will whiten the
hills and shores of the east and the borderless plains of the west,
when the New York and the Newer York of today shall seem to all
future Americans as impossible as they would seem to any Altrurian
now."[39] Although most visitors shared Howells's feeling of enchant-
ment at the White City, this magical vision also awakened in them
a new interest in what design could do for cities and towns all over
America. The tremendous impact made by the Court of Honor was
ample evidence, among other things, of the importance of the landscape architect's chief material—outdoor space. Thus the remarkable
integrative capacity inherent in Olmsted's contribution was in no
small way responsible for the movement that came to be known as
the City Beautiful.[40]

This movement gave coherence, first of all, to the American feeling for urban spaciousness at a time when the street grid of the average city could no longer accommodate increasing traffic. Characterized by a sense of wide-open space and liberating vistas, it was responsible for a striking enlargement of the civic scale of such cities as Chicago, Cleveland, Minneapolis, and Washington, D.C. But the City Beautiful movement extended to architecture as well, taking the Beaux Arts style originally imported from France and incorporating it into American city planning. Throughout the nation, a new interest burgeoned in public buildings, monuments, and civic centers. One new state capitol arose after another in the classical mode, embellished with murals and statues. In the spirit of self-improvement, art museums and libraries were built by the score. One of the reasons for the enormous success of the movement was that it managed to combine lofty ideals of art with the blessing of the business community. The initiative for civic improvement often came from business and professional groups who appreciated an aesthetic sanction for the display of the nation's new wealth.[41]

Renewed Interest in Classical Design

It has been fashionable in recent years to lament that the Chicago fair, with its dedication to the classical tradition, destroyed the possibility of a truly native American architectural style. So thought Louis Sullivan, of the firm of Adler and Sullivan of Chicago, who, without creating overt dissension, flatly disagreed with the fair's classical ideal. Except for the Fisheries Building in the Richardsonian manner by the Chicago architect Henry Ives Cobb, the only exception to the prevailing white, classical pattern was Sullivan's Transportation Building, which stood outside the Court of Honor. This building, with a grand entrance covered with gold leaf, set off by arabesques in orange, red, and yellow stucco, made a highly individual decorative statement that appealed especially to those foreign visitors who hoped to see some innovative architecture comparable to what the European expositions had produced.[42]

Some years later, Sullivan looked back at the Columbian Exposition as an artistic calamity resulting from a "snobbish, alien, imposed culture." Embittered by the decline of his own private practice in the heyday of the classical style that he disliked, he predicted, "The damage wrought by the World's Fair will last for half a century from its date, if not longer."[43] Ironically, however, after a period in which modernism and functionalism have had their own powerful impact on architecture (and in which Sullivan's prediction became a kind of official lament), a renewed interest in classical design is beginning to occur. It is not simply that architectural critics have realized anew what a stunning achievement of the artistic imagination the make-believe palaces and pavilions of 1893 were. These critics are beginning also to reassess the whole classical tradition, finding in it values of wholeness, harmony, and repose that answer a felt need amid the discontent and disorder of society today.

The Chicago fair brought Olmsted to the height of his contemporary fame. In 1893, Harvard and Yale, both of which had awarded him an honorary master of arts degree in 1864, conferred on him the honorary degree of doctor of laws, which he expressed special pleasure in accepting because it gave added standing to his profession of landscape architecture. He was widely praised in newspapers and magazines, including the *Century Illustrated Monthly*, for which Mariana Griswold Van Rensselaer wrote a long, comprehensive, and appreciative account of his career.[44]

Olmsted took considerable satisfaction in having accommodated his talents to a variety of styles and requirements. He saw no necessary conflict between informal and formal schools of design, as exemplified by Central Park and the Chicago fair, the two major urban accomplishments that marked the beginning and conclusion of his career. Though Central Park was, for the most part, romantic in style while the fair was classical and monumental, he assumed there was a place for both. The Chicago fair was essentially architectural, yet he succeeded brilliantly in reconciling a picturesque motif with the formal stateliness that his architectural associates had decided upon for the buildings. Likewise, at Biltmore he managed to reconcile the requirements of Hunt in his French Renaissance chateau with a generally picturesque natural character in its approaches and in the main landscape features.[45] In both instances his use of spatial geometry pointed the way to a more architectonic style than landscaping in America had known up to that time.

Chapter Eight

The Legacy of Frederick Law Olmsted

Paradoxical Position of Olmsted Today

The position of Olmsted today is surely paradoxical. His reputation seems secure, in terms of both the major parks he created and his pioneering achievement on behalf of our state and national park systems. In these efforts alone he is "probably responsible for the betterment and preservation of more of the earth's surface than anyone else."[1] Indeed, in looking over his activities during the latter half of the nineteenth century, we are conscious of Olmsted's having participated directly or indirectly in an incredible number of major projects that influenced aesthetic standards in America.

At the same time, however, when we look hard at most of his creations, we see the disastrous results of neglect, blight, and municipal encroachment. Vandalism and pastoral sabotage have been rampant in Central and Prospect parks. His winding carriage drives through the "emerald necklace" in Boston have become bloated expressways for an auto-industrial age. Parking lots have sprung up in Belle Isle Park, Detroit. Commercial power lines and neon signs have crept up in the vicinity of Niagara Falls. In 1865, Olmsted wrote about the "millions" of visitors that the next century would bring to the then relatively unknown Yosemite. Although he has proved to be prophetic in this prediction, as in many others that he made, he had no way of foreseeing that the Yosemite wilderness today would become partly urbanized, with electrical outlets for campers as well as traffic jams, smog, and crime.

178

Even during Olmsted's own lifetime, his work was seldom treated with the respect he would have liked. Regarding the seventeen large public parks he had designed by 1890, he asserted with a characteristic mixture of pride and regret: "After we have left them, they have in the majority of cases been more or less barbarously treated, yet as they stand . . . they are a hundred years ahead of any spontaneous public demand. . . . And they are having an educative effect perfectly manifest to me—a manifest civilizing effect."[2] These words express something of the complexity of Olmsted's legacy to us. He clearly recognized the prophetic nature of his mission. He had pioneered a new profession and suggested the potential for urban design in America. And, despite the failure of his contemporaries to appreciate what he had done, he never doubted for a moment that he would be vindicated by history. The validity of his belief is corroborated by a modern student of urban landscaping: "The possibilities of master planning and urban design, by which construction and green space could play a gay and variable counterpoint throughout our communities, are just beginning to make some small impact upon our development thinking, though forecast one hundred years ago by Olmsted."[3] Then, too, our present concern with large-scale ecological planning has increased interest in the profession of landscape architecture and has caused us to acknowledge Olmsted as a forerunner of the whole ecological movement.

Yet, to see him as a twentieth-century man would be to miss the distinctive character of his achievements and also to ignore the fact that his way of life has largely disappeared. In stating that his parks were having an educative, "civilizing" effect on his contemporaries, Olmsted revealed himself as a true nineteenth-century man sharing the values of other genteel, conservative reformers of the Gilded Age. It would probably be impossible today to bring back that century's romantic point of view about contemplative landscape pleasures—what architectural critic Ada Louise Huxtable has termed a kind of "existential pastoralism."[4]

It would likewise be difficult to bring back Olmsted's hopes for social improvement through the inspiration of landscape architec-

ture. For his view of the urban park as a civilizing agent was
limited by his age's assumption of benign paternalism within which
his ideas developed. Throughout his career he believed whole-
heartedly in political and social democracy, but his belief was tempered by the proviso that democracy should always be responsive
to a trained and enlightened leadership. In this respect he was
something of an élitist, frequently disturbed by the public's failure
to understand his objectives and to accept his expertise.

Olmsted was enthusiastic about the mingling of all social groups
on his promenades and meadows in furtherance of a democratic
society. He hoped that this alleviation of tensions between rich
and poor would lead to a gradual human improvement. These be-
liefs and hopes seem somewhat naive today in the wake of what
historian Geoffrey Blodgett has called the "aggressive thrust of
American pluralism" in the twentieth century.[5] Such superficial con-
tact between classes has proved to be no substitute for serious
social reform: the problems and resentments of modern urban life
have demanded more direct solutions.

One of the trends in American life that Olmsted did not antici-
pate when he designed Central Park was the growing popularity of
sports and the increasingly physical character of recreation. His emphasis was originally on the pastoral retreat and the pleasure to be
found in viewing a landscape. He provided few opportunities for
vigorous, organized recreation. As public demand for active sports
grew, he was obliged to make greater provision for them. In designing Prospect Park, for example, he created a special Parade Ground
for these activities just outside the park proper, as he created another area for cultural institutions. In the Buffalo system, he advocated a large park for sports on the south side of the city, balancing
his landscaped park on the north. And by the time he designed
Franklin Park in Boston in the 1880s, he kept the broad central area
as a scenic country park but introduced ball diamonds and a fifty-
court tennis field around this rural nucleus.

The playground movement beginning in the 1880s further altered the concept of park design. Recreation equipment, as advocated by reformers like Jacob Riis in New York and Jane Addams

in Chicago, was introduced and gradually became an important feature of many parks. Play equipment in the form of sandboxes, swings, and seesaws was followed by permanent installations for tennis and baseball and, more recently, for swimming. Twenty-seven playgrounds have by now taken bites out of Central Park instead of being accommodated on vest-pocket lots scattered around the perimeter.

Olmsted's Philosophy of Leisure

Although Olmsted himself commented on how "barbarously" most of his parks were treated during his lifetime, it was not until this century that real blight settled over them. By that time the automobile was changing the living patterns and habits of Americans. As the migration to the suburbs from the inner city intensified, so did the neglect of urban parks. More and more Americans began experiencing their rural scenery through a car window. Since then, other contemporary trends have tended to deflect attention from the large city park—the tremendous increase in commercialized spectator entertainment, the greater impoverishment of municipal budgets in the era of the welfare state, and racial and ethnic changes in the big cities, to name just a few. Modern sociology and technology have all but overwhelmed Olmsted's planning vision in an environment in which sound and action often give the appearance of having replaced thought and feeling.[6]

And yet the "civilizing" values that Olmsted cherished would seem to have real contemporary uses, even if they are constantly being eroded by what he would surely think of as twentieth-century barbarism. Although his ideas have been substantially betrayed in most of the places he designed or worked to save, his philosophy of leisure has as much merit today as it did when he first articulated it. Leisure, for him, was what environmentalist Joseph L. Sax has called the "counterpoint of life."[7] It was the occasion for putting the daily routine into perspective, and this opportunity would seem all the more necessary with the increasing pace of urban life in a computerized age. Thus Olmsted believed that the rhythm of nature as found in his parks provides a permanent standard of value and that man can experience this transcendent value by immersing himself in the natural scene, whether in the more limited setting of a Central Park or in the vast reaches of the Yosemite wilderness.

Furthermore, as we have seen, Olmsted had the democratic belief that the experience of quiet solitude in the midst of great natural scenery might induce a state of contemplation in even the most ordinary and uncultivated citizen. This is one of the reasons he exerted so much effort in fighting off various schemes to fill his parks with so-called improvements reflecting the fashions and novelties of the moment. What he wanted, instead, was a natural park that would suggest timelessness, standing outside the scale of urban, man-dominated experience. His philosophy would seem to be borne out by contemporary scientists, who are documenting the importance of nature and natural beauty as a therapeutic antidote to the assaults of daily urban life:

There is an increasing evidence suggesting that mental health and emotional stability of populations may be profoundly influenced by frustrating aspects of an urban, biologically artificial environment. . . . It seems likely that we are genetically programmed to a natural habitat of clean air and a varied green landscape, like any other mammal. . . . The specific physiological reactions to natural beauty and diversity, to the shapes and colors of nature, especially to green, to the motions and sounds of other animals, we do not comprehend and are reluctant to include in studies of environmental quality. Yet it is evident that in our daily lives nature must be thought of not as a luxury to be made available if possible, but as part of our inherent indispensable biological need.[8]

The Continuing Vitality of Central Park

In contrast to the consumer perspective that seems to control contemporary thinking about parks and recreation in general, Olmsted's philosophy points to a broader perspective on the uses of leisure. He realized the crucial importance of preserving a link to the natural forces that would ensure mental health and emotional stability—natural forces that could change the pace of life and permit the seasonal rhythms of his parks to take over.⁹ And, despite the dilapidation and ill-use of Olmsted's parks today, these rhythms are still very much in evidence. Central Park, for example, somehow manages to function as vitally as it did in the nineteenth century. Even though its physical condition is abominable, it still ranks high in the affection of many New Yorkers. There is an essence that endures, and that essence may even be a kind of salvation for New York City.

Central Park helps to humanize the city's hardness. On any pleasant Sunday, thousands of New Yorkers shake off their paranoia and enjoy themselves in the park in a multitude of ways. The steady stream of bicyclists and joggers on the park drives, from which cars are now banned on weekends, represents a cross section of the city's classes, races, and cultures that provides a concrete image of what a truly democratic community might be like. The urban tensions of which Olmsted spoke so often seem to be diminished, whether through the tranquillity of a picnic on the grass or through the rough-and-tumble of an organized athletic contest in which racial and ethnic differences seem magically to dissolve for the moment. And the park still provides recreation, as Olmsted foresaw, for those who have no other escape on weekends, for many who feel the pressures of poverty or apathy. There, despite the risk of a mugging, everyone has open space in which to express himself, rather than confined space in which to be acted upon—the normal, daily experience of many New Yorkers.

The original design of Central Park by Olmsted and Vaux has proved ingenious and flexible enough to accommodate the changing nature of recreational activities through the years. In recent decades, for example, the Sheep Meadow at the heart of the park has been used for concerts, operas, theater, and a variety of "happenings." The crowds are heavier today than ever before. Those preservationists who would like to restore the park to Olmsted's original vision of pastoral order deplore the fact that, the more use the park gets, the farther it drifts from that vision. Yet it is evident that, in a modern city alive with tensions and raging with large social issues, Central Park is inevitably going to reflect the times.

Like Central Park, all the other Olmsted parks today show the strain of adapting to new conditions, and by comparison, New York appears to have made better use of its parks, and to have dealt with their problems more sensitively, than many other cities. With some of these parks, the problem has been overdevelopment. In others, like Franklin Park in Boston, there has been a serious falling off in use. This park was created as Boston's great rural pleasure ground and functioned as such for many years. Gradually, however, it has become caught in social circumstances that have attached it to a single community rather than continuing it as a city-wide resource. As the middle-class residents of the area in which Franklin Park is located moved to the suburbs, their place was taken by the urban poor, and the park has suffered greatly as a result.[10]

Another Olmsted design, Delaware Park in Buffalo, has experienced traumatic change in the last few decades with the construction of an expressway and interchanges that have bisected the entire park area and drastically altered the landscape. When the city of Buffalo awoke to the enormity of what it had allowed to happen, it became the first American city to draw up a complete master plan for its central park, something even New York City has never been able to achieve despite the obvious need. It seems significant that, in no case involving an Olmsted park, has there been serious discussion of giving up the park land altogether. No major proposals have been presented for abandoning entirely the character of a major park as a landscaped oasis. Under way in Buffalo, instead, is a major effort, undertaken by citizens' advisory groups working closely with professional planners, to accommodate to modern conditions a park planned according to a nineteenth-century philosophy.[11]

An Organic Approach to Landscape Design

Another important legacy of Olmsted is his organic approach to landscape planning—an approach that takes into account both aesthetic and social dimensions of the job at hand. A remarkable feature of his career was not only the designs he formulated but the balance and inclusiveness of his day-to-day decisions. It is true that his principle of finding the controlling idea for a design in its context was not new: it was at the heart of the tradition of English naturalistic landscape design, which was a strong influence on him. But he made a practice of insisting upon it in whatever he did. He was determined to counteract the prevalent idea that a landscape architect was simply a glorified gardener employed to decorate a piece of ground after it had already been developed. He always found the controlling idea for a job at the very beginning. General aims and ends of a plan were fully discussed before it was executed, and sometimes the job a client called for was not at all, in Olmsted's opinion, the job that should be done.

A good example of his approach was the project at Biltmore. George Washington Vanderbilt had wanted some sort of country park as a setting for his vast chateau, but Olmsted discovered that the soil was too thin and the topography generally unsuitable. Here, instead, he found his controlling idea in a smaller park and gardens that would lead into a demonstration forest preserve run according to the practice of scientific forestry. Thus a beautiful rural retreat came to be laid out with economic, educational, and scientific advantages—the kinds of "civilizing" values that were always a part of his thinking.

After Olmsted had found the controlling idea for a job, he then tried to make every element of the design contribute to that idea. Since he was working with space, he continually had to do battle with those who saw his parks as so much cheap, "empty" land on which to load features and activities incongruous with what he felt parks should be. He always emphasized the integrity of his parks as works of art, with all their elements uniting in organic designs. For this reason, he resisted attempts to fill the empty spaces with buildings and monuments other than those warranted for park purposes. Similarly, he insisted that wilderness parks like Yosemite were more than simply undestroyed scenery to serve the popular taste for convenience that cities had spawned. He never lost sight of his principle that parks were to be designed to accommodate large numbers of people without depriving them of the kinds of experiences for which the areas had been created.

Another remarkable aspect of Olmsted's career was his ability to combine the talents of artist and organizer—talents that are frequently mutually exclusive. He was a visionary and at the same time a highly efficient, sometimes imperious manager with the ability to solve large problems and yet pay attention to small details. The transformation of Central Park's wasteland of rocks, swamps, and barren pastures, for example, required the movement of millions of cubic yards of stone and earth with pick and shovel, horse and cart. Olmsted personally supervised all the details of this project, becoming what the contemporary artist Robert Smithson has called "America's first 'earthwork artist.' "[12]

Pioneer City Planner

Olmsted's role as a pioneer city planner is significant as another legacy. Although he began his series of careers as a scientific farmer, he soon came to the conclusion that the nation's destiny lay with the cities, not the country. Well aware of the pressures and even disasters of nineteenth-century urban growth, he nevertheless came to look upon cities as the great civilizing agencies of the modern world—places of communication and vocational specialization among men and women. His urban parks were as important for their urbanity as for their rusticity, and he spent much of his career as a landscape architect working out the symbiotic relationship he felt should exist between city and country.

The totality of the city, its functions and its improvement, became increasingly important to him. During his long association with New York City, he came as close to being a master planner as the city has ever had. The report he wrote for the Brooklyn park commissioners in 1866 contained plans for the entire region, with connecting, tree-lined boulevards from the Atlantic beaches, through the most attractive parts of the cities of Brooklyn and New York, to the Hudson River. Olmsted considered all of his landscape parks, parkways, and urban and suburban areas as integral parts of his comprehensive metropolitan ideal. New York City has still not caught up with this vision.

Olmsted's professional experience in Boston proved to be much less stormy than that in New York. There he was able to do what he had only dreamed about earlier: to lay out the nation's first metropolitan-scale park and parkway system. At the very time that he was being forced out of his job on Central Park, Boston was ready to engage him in what was to become its famous seven-mile "emerald necklace" of open space. Its enlightened social and political environment, as well as its peculiar topography, helped him to accomplish much in the way of park and city planning that had frustrated him in New York. The Boston greenbelt system, following both topography and residential growth from city center to suburbs, offered him the opportunity to carry out his boldest design and his most comprehensive urban planning. It was not just formal and physical toward the creation of a beautiful city, but also social in his continuing concern for pleasant, healthful living arrangements for city and suburban dwellers.

Educator of Leading Landscape Architects

Finally, Olmsted left a rich legacy for the future in the extraordinary training he gave others in the field of landscape architecture. By means of a thorough system of apprenticeship in his office in Brookline, he helped educate many of those who would become leading landscape architects—among them Henry Sargent Codman, Charles Eliot, Arthur Shurcliff, and Frederick Law Olmsted, Jr. Thus he perpetuated his views on design well into the present century. He perpetuated also, through his apprentices, his strong sense of social idealism, his concern for the broad range of human possibility. For he was, throughout his career, a magnanimous man who could be counted on to place public welfare ahead of private welfare. In the midst of his success in creating Central Park, for instance, he had responded immediately to the Confederate attack on Fort Sumter in 1861: he decided to leave his park work and accept a call to serve as executive secretary of the newly created Sanitary Commission, precursor of the American Red Cross.

Tragically, the premature deaths of Codman and Eliot in the 1890s removed two of the ablest practitioners of landscape architecture. But despite the meager numbers, eleven charter members met in 1899 to form the first professional association of landscape architects, the American Society of Landscape Architects. Included were: John Charles Olmsted, a partner in the Olmsted firm since 1884; Frederick Law Olmsted, Jr., who had joined his elder half brother John in partnership in 1898; Samuel Parsons, Jr., a former partner of Calvert Vaux who was now landscape architect to the recently enlarged city of New York; Warren H. Manning, another of Olmsted's early apprentices, who had just opened his own office in Boston; Downing Vaux, son of Calvert Vaux who had worked with his father from the middle 1880s until 1895; and Beatrix Cadwalader Jones, who had studied under Charles Sprague Sargent at the Arnold Arboretum.

The fact that six of the eleven charter members were associated in some way with Olmsted and his career suggests how much Olmsted had dominated the profession. One year later, in 1900, Harvard University established the first university curriculum of professional training in landscape architecture in America. This was a memorial to Charles Eliot. President Eliot, his father, selected Frederick Law Olmsted, Jr., to organize and head the program.[13] In this way, as in many others, the influence of one of the great and catalytic movers of the nineteenth century was to pass on far into the twentieth.

Notes and References

Preface

1. *Garden and Forest: A Journal of Horticulture, Landscape Art, and Forestry* 6 (3 May 1893): 192.

Chapter One

1. Olmsted to Parke Godwin, 1 August 1858, Bryant-Godwin papers, Manuscript Division, New York Public Library.
2. John Hull Olmsted to Olmsted, 13 November 1857, Frederick Law Olmsted papers.
3. Laura Wood Roper, *FLO: A Biography of Frederick Law Olmsted* (Baltimore, 1973), p. 215.
4. Olmsted to Henry Whitney Bellows, 13 August 1863, Frederick Law Olmsted papers.
5. Frederick Law Olmsted, "The Yosemite Valley and the Mariposa Big Trees: A Preliminary Report (1865)," with an introductory note by Laura Wood Roper, *Landscape Architecture* 43 (October 1952): 16.
6. Carl P. Russell, *One Hundred Years in Yosemite: The Story of a Great Park and Its Friends* (Berkeley, 1947), p. 149.

Chapter Two

1. Olmsted to John Hull Olmsted, 23 June 1845, Frederick Law Olmsted papers.
2. "Appeal to the Citizens of Staten Island," December 1849.
3. *Walks and Talks of an American Farmer in England,* introd. Alex L. Murray (Ann Arbor: University of Michigan Press, 1967), p. 52.
4. Ibid., pp. 52, 54.

5. *A Journey in the Back Country*, introd. Clement Eaton (New York: Schocken Books, 1970), p. 6.

6. *Democracy in America*, ed. Phillips Bradley (New York: Alfred A. Knopf, 1945), I, 365.

7. *Back Country*, p. 446.

8. Ibid., p. 447.

9. Ibid., p. 7.

10. *A Journey in the Seaboard Slave States*, p. 177.

11. *New-York Daily Times*, 3 March 1854.

12. Laura Wood Roper, "Frederick Law Olmsted and the Western Texas Free-Soil Movement," *American Historical Review* 56 (1950): 61–62.

13. *Back Country*, p. 7.

14. Ibid., p. 9.

15. Laura Wood Roper, "Frederick Law Olmsted in the 'Literary Republic,'" *Mississippi Valley Historical Review* 39 (1952): 478–79.

16. Olmsted to Charles Loring Brace, 8 December 1860, Frederick Law Olmsted papers.

17. *The Cotton Kingdom*, ed. Arthur M. Schlesinger (New York: Alfred A. Knopf, 1953), p. 5.

18. Ibid., p. 4.

19. Roper, "Frederick Law Olmsted in the 'Literary Republic,'" pp. 480–81.

20. Letter to Olmsted from Lowell, 25 January 1862, Frederick Law Olmsted papers.

21. Olmsted to Charles Loring Brace, 18 November 1861, Frederick Law Olmsted papers.

22. "The Rebellion. How to Reason with the South. How to Deal with the Slavery Question," *New York Times*, 4 December 1861.

23. Letter to Thomas H. Clark, 5 August 1889, in Clark's "Frederick Law Olmsted on the South, 1889," *South Atlantic Quarterly* 3 (1904): 11–15.

24. F. Scott Fitzgerald, *The Crack-Up*, ed. Edmund Wilson (New York: New Directions, 1956), p. 69.

25. *Back Country*, p. 9.

26. *Time on the Cross* (Boston, 1974).

27. *Patriotic Gore: Studies in the Literature of the American Civil War* (New York: Oxford University Press, 1962), p. 221.

28. *Seaboard Slave States,* pp. 501–2.

29. Ibid.

30. *The Cotton Kingdom,* p. 619.

31. *New-York Daily Times,* 12 January 1854.

32. *Landscape into Cityscape: Frederick Law Olmsted's Plans for a Greater New York City,* introd. Albert Fein (Ithaca: Cornell University Press, 1967), pp. 20–21.

33. William Harper, *Memoir on Slavery* (Charleston, S.C., 1838), p. 53.

34. Olmsted to Parke Godwin, 1 August 1858, Bryant-Godwin papers, Manuscript Division, New York Public Library.

Chapter Three

1. Frederick Law Olmsted, Jr. and Theodora Kimball, eds., *Forty Years of Landscape Architecture: Frederick Law Olmsted, Sr.,* 2 vols. (New York: G. P. Putnam's, 1922), 2:35.

2. Olmsted, Jr., and Kimball, pp. 41–42.

3. *New York Times,* 30 April 1858.

4. Olmsted, Jr., and Kimball, p. 214.

5. Ibid., p. 44.

6. *New York Times,* 11 November 1858.

7. Olmsted, Jr., and Kimball, p. 74.

8. Ibid.

9. Ibid., p. 79.

10. *Landscape into Cityscape,* p. 98.

11. Ibid., p. 108.

12. Ibid., p. 99.

13. Olmsted, Jr., and Kimball, p. 92.

14. *Landscape into Cityscape,* p. 334.

15. Ibid., p. 363.

16. Olmsted to Charles Loring Brace, 7 March 1882, Frederick Law Olmsted papers.

17. *Landscape into Cityscape,* p. 438.

18. Olmsted to Calvert Vaux, 9 July 1887, Frederick Law Olmsted papers.

19. Olmsted to William A. Stiles, 10 March 1895, Frederick Law Olmsted papers.

Chapter Four

1. *Civilizing American Cities: A Selection of Frederick Law Olmsted's Writings on City Landscapes,* ed. S. B. Sutton (Cambridge, Mass. 1971), p. 115.

2. Ibid., p. 117.

3. Roper, p. 317.

4. *Landscape into Cityscape,* p. 100.

5. Elizabeth Stevenson, *Park Maker: A Life of Frederick Law Olmsted* (New York, 1977), p. 281.

6. *Civilizing American Cities,* p. 293.

7. Ibid., p. 292.

8. Ibid., p. 300.

9. Ibid., p. 162.

10. Ibid., pp. 162–63.

11. Roper, p. 322.

12. A. L. Murray, "Frederick Law Olmsted and the Design of Mount Royal Park, Montreal," *Journal of the Society of Architectural Historians* 26 (1967): 166.

13. *Civilizing American Cities,* pp. 209, 211.

14. Ibid., p. 212, n.

15. Ibid., p. 214.

16. Ibid.

17. Ibid., p. 56.

18. Ibid., p. 65.

19. Ibid., p. 78.

20. Ibid., p. 80.

21. Roper, p. 329.

22. Julius G. Fabos, Gordon T. Milde, and V. Michael Weinmayr, *Frederick Law Olmsted, Sr.: Founder of Landscape Architecture in America* (Amherst, 1968), pp. 57–58.

23. Norman T. Newton, *Design on the Land: The Development of Landscape Architecture* (Cambridge, Mass. 1971), pp. 295–96.

24. Ibid., p. 298.

25. Ibid., p. 299.

26. Fabos, pp. 58–59.

27. Geoffrey Blodgett, "Frederick Law Olmsted: Landscape Architecture as Conservative Reform," *Journal of American History* 62 (1976): 883–85.

28. Newton, pp. 301, 304.

29. Olmsted to his partners, 28 October 1893, Frederick Law Olmsted papers.

Chapter Five

1. *Civilizing American Cities,* p. 265.

2. Ibid., pp. 288–89.

3. Olmsted, Vaux and Company, *A Few Things To Be Thought of Before Proceeding to Plan Buildings for the National Agricultural Colleges* (New York: American News Company, 1866), pp. 9–22.

4. Roper, pp. 313–14.

5. Olmsted, Vaux and Company, *Architect's Report to the Board of Trustees of the College of Agriculture and the Mechanic Arts, of the State of Maine,* 46th Legislature, House Document no. 57 (1867), pp. 22, 28.

6. Ibid., pp. 18, 24.

7. Roper, p. 321.

8. Ibid., pp. 367–68.

9. *Report of the New Capitol Commission Relative to the Plans Submitted by Messrs. Frederick Law Olmsted, Leopold Eidlitz, and H. H. Richardson* (State of New York, Senate, March 3, 1876), no. 49, pp. 6, 14–15; Montgomery Schuyler, "The Capitol of New York," *Scribner's Monthly Magazine,* 19 (December, 1879), 161–178.

10. Roper, pp. 370–71; Schuyler, p. 166.

11. *American Architect and Building News* 5 (18 January 1879): 29.

12. Roper, pp. 373–75.

13. Roper, p. 376; *Annual Report of the Architect of the Capitol for the Year Ending June 30, 1882,* pp. 15–16.

14. Olmsted to George E. Waring, Jr., 19 July 1874, Frederick Law Olmsted papers.

15. Roper, p. 377.

16. Charles C. McLaughlin, "The Capitol in Peril? The West Front Controversy from Walter to Stewart," *Records of the Columbia Historical Society of Washington, D.C., 1969–70* (Washington, D.C., 1971), pp. 241–46.

17. Roper, pp. 378, 399.

18. Ibid., pp. 406–7.

19. Olmsted to Charles Eliot, 20 July 1886, Frederick Law Olmsted papers.

20. Roper, p. 408; George T. Clark, *Leland Stanford, War Governor of California, Railroad Builder and Founder of Stanford University* (Stanford, 1931), pp. 401–3.

21. Olmsted to Leland Stanford, 27 November 1886, Frederick Law Olmsted papers.

22. Roper, p. 411; Diane K. McGuire, "Early Site Planning on the West Coast: Frederick Law Olmsted's Plan for Stanford University," *Landscape Architecture* 47 (January 1957): 346–47.

23. Fabos, pp. 75–76.

24. Charles A. Coolidge to Olmsted, 3 May 1887, Frederick Law Olmsted papers.

25. Stevenson, p. 382.

26. McGuire, p. 349; Roper, pp. 412–14.

27. McGuire, p. 349.

28. Fabos, pp. 76–77.

Chapter Six

1. Olmsted to Mary C. Olmsted, 20 November 1863, Frederick Law Olmsted papers.

2. Frederick Law Olmsted, "The Yosemite Valley and the Mariposa Big Trees: A Preliminary Report (1865)," with an introductory note by Laura Wood Roper, *Landscape Architect* 43 (October 1952): 16.

3. Hans Huth, "Yosemite: The Story of an Idea," *Sierra Club Bulletin* 33 (March 1948): 66–68.

4. Joseph L. Sax, "America's National Parks: Their Principles, Purposes, and Prospects," *Natural History Special Supplement,* October 1976, p. 65.

5. Ibid., pp. 61, 59–60.

6. Olmsted, "The Yosemite Valley," p. 12.

7. Roper, p. 287.

8. Ibid., p. 285.

9. Huth, p. 52.

10. Sax, pp. 71, 64–65.

11. Ibid., p. 74.

12. Olmsted, "The Yosemite Valley," pp. 13–25.

13. Charles C. McLaughlin, ed., *The Papers of Frederick Law Olmsted*, Vol. 1, *The Formative Years: 1822–1852* (Baltimore, 1977), p. 32.

14. Stevenson, p. 288.

15. Olmsted, "The Yosemite Valley," p. 13.

16. McLaughlin, p. 32.

17. Stevenson, pp. 288, 392–93.

18. Newton, pp. 522, 558.

19. Hans Huth, *Nature and the American: Three Centuries of Changing Attitudes* (Berkeley, 1957), p. 150.

20. Sax, p. 64.

21. Roper, p. 379.

22. Albert Fein, *Frederick Law Olmsted and the American Environmental Tradition* (New York, 1972), p. 42.

23. *Special Report of the New York State Survey on the Preservation of the Scenery of Niagara Falls, and Fourth Annual Report on the Triangulation of the State for the Year 1879*, p. 7.

24. Roper, p. 380.

25. *Special Report of the New York State Survey*, pp. 31–39.

26. Roper, p. 381.

27. Ibid., pp. 382, 395.

28. Ibid., p. 396.

29. Jonathan Baxter Harrison, "Charles Eliot Norton and Niagara Falls," Norton papers, Library of Congress.

30. Roper, p. 397.

31. Frederick Law Olmsted, "Governmental Preservation of Natural Scenery" (pamphlet), Brookline, Mass., 8 March 1890.

32. Sax, pp. 78–79.

33. Mariana Griswold Van Rensselaer, *Henry Hobson Richardson and His Works* (Boston, 1888), p. 118.

34. Olmsted, "Governmental Preservation of Natural Scenery."

Chapter Seven

1. Olmsted to Frederick J. Kingsbury, 20 January 1891, Frederick Law Olmsted papers.

2. Roper, p. 415.

3. Ibid., p. 416.

4. Newton, pp. 339–46.

5. Newton, pp. 346–49; Olmsted to Richard Morris Hunt, 2 March 1889, Frederick Law Olmsted papers.

6. Olmsted to George W. Vanderbilt, 12 July 1889, Frederick Law Olmsted papers.

7. Stevenson, p. 404.

8. Newton, p. 347.

9. Olmsted to George W. Vanderbilt, 12 July 1889, Frederick Law Olmsted papers.

10. Newton, p. 348.

11. Roper, p. 418.

12. Ibid., pp. 417–19.

13. Gifford Pinchot, *Breaking New Ground* (New York: Harcourt Brace, 1947), p. 15.

14. Ibid., p. 48.

15. Roper, p. 419; Pinchot, pp. 48–49.

16. Stevenson, p. 405; Newton, p. 351.

17. Roper, pp. 417, 455, 465–66, 477; Olmsted to Charles S. Sargent, 25 April 1895, Frederick Law Olmsted papers.

18. Olmsted to his partners, 1 November 1893, Frederick Law Olmsted papers.

19. Stevenson, p. 389; Newton, p. 351.

20. Frederick Law Olmsted, "A Report Upon the Landscape Architecture of the Columbian Exposition to the American Institute of Architects," pp. 6–7, 9, 11.

21. Olmsted to John Charles Olmsted, 24 November 1890, Frederick Law Olmsted papers.

22. Newton, p. 357.

23. F. L. Olmsted and Co., John W. Root, and D. H. Burnham, *Report to Joint Committee on Site* (Chicago, 1890), pp. 10–12.

24. Frederick Law Olmsted, "The Landscape Architecture of the World's Columbian Exposition," *Proceedings of the 27th Annual Convention of the A.I.A.* (Chicago, 1893), p. 163.

25. Newton, p. 359.

26. Fabos, p. 91.

27. Charles Moore, *Daniel Hudson Burnham, Architect, Planner of Cities* (Boston, 1921), 1:47.

28. Newton, pp. 362–63.

29. Frederick Law Olmsted, "Memorandum as to What is to be Aimed at in the Planting of the Lagoon District of the Chicago Exposition, as Proposed March, 1891," *American Florist* 11 (January 1896): 602–4.

30. Olmsted to Daniel H. Burnham, 23, 28 December 1891, Frederick Law Olmsted papers.

31. Olmsted to his partners, 17 July 1892, Frederick Law Olmsted papers.

32. Victoria Post Ranney, *Olmsted in Chicago* (Chicago, 1972), pp. 37–38.

33. Olmsted, "Report Upon the Landscape Architecture," p. 14.

34. Stevenson, p. 398.

35. Moore, 1: 74.

36. Ibid., 1: 78–79.

37. Olmsted to D. H. Burnham, 20 June 1893, Frederick Law Olmsted papers.

38. Newton, pp. 365, 367.

39. William Dean Howells, *The Altrurian Romances,* ed. Clara and Rudolf Kirk (Bloomington: Indiana University Press, 1968), p. 198.

40. Newton, p. 370.

41. August Heckscher, *Open Spaces: The Life of American Cities* (New York, 1977), pp. 19–24.

42. Wayne Andrews, *Architecture, Ambition, and Americans: A Social History of American Architecture,* rev. ed. (New York, 1978), p. 214; Newton, p. 370.

43. Louis Sullivan, *The Autobiography of an Idea* (New York: Press of the A.I.A., 1924), p. 325.

44. Roper, pp. 450–52.

45. Olmsted to W. A. Stiles, 10 March 1895, Frederick Law Olmsted papers.

Chapter Eight

1. Elizabeth Barlow and William Alex, *Frederick Law Olmsted's New York* (New York, 1972), pp. 54, 56.

2. Olmsted to Mrs. William Dwight Whitney, 16 December 1890, Frederick Law Olmsted papers.

3. Garrett Eckbo, *Urban Landscape Design* (New York, 1964), p. 99.

4. Ada Louise Huxtable, "It Isn't Green Cheese," *New York Times,* 21 May 1972, sec. 2, p. 25.

5. Blodgett, p. 889.

6. Ibid., pp. 887–88.

7. Sax, pp. 76–77.

8. Hugh H. Iltis, Orie L. Loucks, and Peter Andrews, "Criteria for an Optimum Human Environment," *Science and Public Affairs* 26 (1970): 2–6.

9. Sax, pp. 79–81.

10. Heckscher, pp. 172, 182–84.

11. Ibid., pp. 180–81.

12. Robert Smithson, "Frederick Law Olmsted and the Dialectical Landscape," *Artforum* 11 (1973): 65.

13. Newton, pp. 336, 385–91.

Selected Bibliography

PRIMARY SOURCES

The Frederick Law Olmsted papers (61 containers; 24,000 items) and supplementary papers of Olmsted Associates, Inc., and its predecessors (650 containers; 170,000 items) are located in the Manuscript Division, Library of Congress, Washington, D.C. The Calvert Vaux papers are located in the Manuscripts and Archives Division, New York Public Library, Astor, Lenox and Tilden Foundations. The Olmsted-Vaux plan for Central Park is located in the Arsenal, Central Park, New York City.

Walks and Talks of an American Farmer in England. New York: G. P. Putnam, 1852.

A Journey in the Seaboard Slave States, with Remarks on Their Economy. New York: Dix, Edwards, 1856.

A Journey Through Texas; or, A Saddle-Trip on the Southwestern Frontier. New York: Dix, Edwards, 1857.

A Journey in the Back Country. New York: Mason Brothers, 1860.

The Cotton Kingdom: A Traveller's Observations on Cotton and Slavery in the American Slave States. 2 vols. New York: Mason Brothers, 1861.

Public Parks and the Enlargement of Towns. Read before the American Social Science Association at the Lowell Institute, Boston, Massachusetts, February 25, 1870. Printed at the Riverside Press, Cambridge, Massachusetts, 1870.

The Spoils of the Park, with a Few Leaves from the Deep-Laden Note-Books of "A Wholly Unpractical Man." Detroit, Mich. 1882.

"The Yosemite Valley and the Mariposa Big Trees: A Preliminary Report, 1865." Reproduced with an introductory note by Laura Wood Roper. *Landscape Architecture* 43 (October 1952): 12–25.

Landscape into Cityscape: Frederick Law Olmsted's Plans for a Greater New York City. Edited with an introductory essay by Albert Fein. Ithaca: Cornell University Press, 1967.

Frederick Law Olmsted, Landscape Architect, 1822–1903. Edited by Frederick Law Olmsted, Jr., and Theodora Kimball. 2 vols. in 1. New York: Benjamin Blom, 1970. Original edition, 1922, 1928.

Civilizing American Cities: A Selection of Frederick Law Olmsted's Writings on City Landscapes. Edited by S. B. Sutton. Cambridge, Mass.: MIT Press, 1971.

The Papers of Frederick Law Olmsted. Vol. 1. *The Formative Years, 1822 to 1852.* Edited by Charles Capen McLaughlin. Baltimore: Johns Hopkins University Press, 1977.

SECONDARY SOURCES

Allen, B. Sprague. *Tides in English Taste.* Cambridge: Harvard University Press, 1937. A background of the history of art for the study of literature, 1619–1800, with special attention to the development of garden design.

Andrews, Wayne. *Architecture, Ambition, and Americans.* Rev. ed. New York: Free Press, 1978. A social history of American architecture as a fine art, with separate sections on Richard Morris Hunt and the World's Columbian Exposition.

Barlow, Elizabeth. *The Central Park Book.* New York: Central Park Task Force, 1977. Describes how Central Park can encompass a broad range of recreational activities and can also be a learning laboratory for such subjects as geology, botany, and ornithology.

————, and Alex, William. *Frederick Law Olmsted's New York.* Illustrative portfolio by William Alex. New York: Praeger Publishers, in association with the Whitney Museum of American Art, 1972. Published in connection with a major exhibition, organized by William Alex at the Whitney Museum in 1972, to mark the 150th anniversary of Olmsted's birth.

Blodgett, Geoffrey. "Frederick Law Olmsted: Landscape Architecture as Conservative Reform." *Journal of American History* 62 (March 1976): 869–89. Traces the continuities in Olmsted's conservative social attitudes from his journalistic days to his profession of landscape architecture.

Brooks, Van Wyck. *The Flowering of New England, 1815–1865.* New York: E. P. Dutton, 1937. The first of Brooks's volumes sketching the literary history of the United States, focusing on the New England mind as discernible in the lives and works of its writers.

————. *The World of Washington Irving.* Philadelphia: Blakiston, 1945. Precedes *The Flowering of New England* historically and provides background on Philadelphia, New York, New England, the South, and the West in the early years of the nineteenth century.

Burchard, John, and Bush-Brown, Albert. *The Architecture of America.* Boston: Little, Brown, 1961. The impact of our changing American society on the profession of architecture, the book sponsored by the American Institute of Architects.

Callow, Alexander B., Jr. "The Crusade Against the Tweed Ring." In *American Urban History: An Interpretive Reader with Commentaries,* edited by Alexander B. Callow, Jr. New York: Oxford University Press, 1969. An analysis of one of the most notorious political organizations in American urban history, which helped drive Olmsted from his New York City park work.

Callow, James T. *Kindred Spirits: Knickerbocker Writers and American Artists, 1807–1855.* Chapel Hill: University of North Carolina Press, 1967. Traces the unusually close relationship between the visual and the literary arts during the first half of the nineteenth century.

Caro, Robert A. *The Power Broker: Robert Moses and the Fall of New York.* New York: Alfred A. Knopf, 1974. Concerns Robert Moses and the hidden story behind the shaping of modern New York, including the neglect that has often characterized Central Park since Olmsted's time.

Cecil, William A. V. *Biltmore: The Vision and Reality of George W. Vanderbilt, Richard Morris Hunt, and Frederick Law Olmsted.* Asheville, N.C.: Biltmore Estate, 1972. A detailed photographic study of one of Olmsted's great collaborative efforts.

Chadwick, George F. *The Park and the Town: Public Landscape in the 19th and 20th Centuries.* New York: Praeger, 1966. Treats the public park as one of the main contributions of the Victorians to urban life, including ample discussion of the American Park Movement.

Clark, George T. *Leland Stanford: War Governor of California, Railroad Builder, and Founder of Stanford University.* Stanford: Stanford University Press, 1931. A detailed biography of the pioneer American builder, who engaged Olmsted to plan the campus of Stanford University.

Creese, Walter L. *The Search for Environment.* New Haven: Yale University Press, 1966. The cultural implications of the English garden city, with some attention to Olmsted's suburb of Riverside.

Donald, David. *Charles Sumner and the Coming of the Civil War.* New York: Alfred A. Knopf, 1960. The biography of a man whose life touched on almost every significant movement in mid-nineteenth-century American history.

Downing, Andrew Jackson. *The Architecture of Country Houses, Including Designs for Cottages, Farm Houses, and Villas.* New York: D. Appleton, 1850. The enormously popular nineteenth-century book expressing Downing's prescriptions for the most appropriate houses and furnishings for ideal American living.

_____. *A Treatise on the Theory and Practice of Landscape Gardening, Adapted to North America, with a View to the Improvement of Country Residences.* New York: George P. Putnam, 1853. Laments the fact that professional talent was seldom employed in the landscape gardens of his time and presents principles for the ornamentation of private grounds.

Eckbo, Garrett. *Urban Landscape Design.* New York: McGraw-Hill, 1964. Concerned with the quality of the physical landscape in which we live, acknowledging the farsighted thinking of Olmsted in such features as parks and playgrounds.

Eliot, Charles W. *Charles Eliot, Landscape Architect.* Boston: Houghton Mifflin, 1902. A detailed biography, written by Eliot's father, of one of Olmsted's leading protégés.

Fabos, Julius G., Milde, Gordon T., and Weinmayr, V. Michael. *Frederick Law Olmsted, Sr.: Founder of Landscape Architecture in America.* Amherst: University of Massachusetts Press, 1968. Published in connection with a national traveling exhibition of Olmsted's work, presented under the auspices of the American Society of Landscape Architects and the Harvard Graduate School of Design.

Fein, Albert. *Frederick Law Olmsted and the American Environmental Tradition.* New York: George Braziller, 1972. Explains and illustrates the relevance of Olmsted's life and planning to the current racial, urban, and ecological crises affecting the United States.

Fitch, James M. *Architecture and the Esthetics of Plenty.* New York: Columbia University Press, 1961. A collection of diversified essays, including two of special relevance to Olmsted: on Louis Sullivan and on the American pleasure garden.

Fogel, Robert W., and Engerman, Stanley L. *Time on the Cross: The Economics of American Negro Slavery.* Boston: Little, Brown, 1974. A reexamination of the economic foundations of American Negro slavery, challenging virtually every traditional assumption about the slaves in the antebellum South.

Genovese, Eugene D. *Roll, Jordan, Roll: The World the Slaves Made.* New York: Pantheon Books, 1974. Finds Olmsted a scrupulous observer of slave conditions in the Old South during the 1850s.

Giedion, Sigfried. *Space, Time and Architecture.* Cambridge: Harvard University Press, 1941. The growth of a new tradition in architecture, showing its interrelationship with other human activities such as construction, painting, city planning, and science.

Hamlin, Talbot. *Architecture Through the Ages.* New York: G. P. Putnam's, 1940. A comprehensive history of the architecture of the Western World, especially useful for its chapters on "The Classic Revival in the United States" and "Eclecticism."

Harris, Neil. *The Artist in American Society: The Formative Years 1790–1860.* New York: George Braziller, 1966. A study of American artists and their place in the cultural life of the nation during the first half of the nineteenth century.

Heckscher, August. *Open Spaces: The Life of American Cities.* New York: Harper and Row, 1977. Deals with the uses of urban open space, with ample coverage of the conflicts between those who would return to the romantic park landscapes Olmsted envisioned and others who support new uses for parks.

Heidrich, Robert W. *Riverside: A Village in a Park.* Riverside, Ill.: Frederick Law Olmsted Society, 1970. A brief history of the nation's first significant planned suburb, published by the Olmsted Society of Riverside to commemorate the village's designation as a National Historic Landmark in 1970.

Hitchcock, Henry-Russell. *The Architecture of H. H. Richardson and his Times.* 3d ed. Cambridge: MIT Press, 1966. Not a complete biography of Olmsted's colleague and friend but rather a study of his architecture in the light of the environment in which he worked.

Hoffmann, Donald. *The Architecture of John Wellborn Root*. Baltimore: Johns Hopkins University Press, 1973. The life and work of the Chicago architect, whose contribution to the World's Columbian Exposition was limited because of his untimely death.

Howat, John K. *The Hudson River and its Painters*. New York: Viking, 1972. The landscape painters of the Hudson River School as one of the most important contributions to the development of American artistic tradition.

Hubbard, Henry V., and Kimball, Theodora. *An Introduction to the Study of Landscape Design*. New York: Macmillan, 1917. An aesthetic theory used as the basis of an organization of the field of landscape design, with special attention to landscape parks and reservations.

Huth, Hans. *Nature and the American: Three Centuries of Changing Attitudes*. Berkeley: University of California Press, 1957. Traces the developments leading to the conservation movement in the United States, suggesting that these developments were both causes and effects of changes in the American point of view regarding nature.

Huxtable, Ada Louise. "Up in Central Park." *New York Times*, 19 March 1967. An account of the lack of judgment and taste that has consistently characterized attempts to "improve" Central Park.

Jackson, John B. *American Space: The Centennial Years, 1865–1876*. New York: Norton, 1972. The technological, social, and aesthetic transformations of the rural and urban landscape in various regions of the United States during the crucial decade following the Civil War.

Kaufmann, Edgar, Jr., ed. *The Rise of an American Architecture*. New York: Praeger Publishers, in association with the Metropolitan Museum of Art, 1970. Essays on the contribution of nineteenth-century America to the history of architecture and city planning, published in conjunction with the 1970 Centennial exhibition at the Metropolitan Museum of Art.

Loudon, John C. *The Landscape Gardening and Landscape Architecture of Humphry Repton, Esq.* London: Longman, 1840. Repton's general principles of landscape gardening, followed by an application to the laying out of country residences and public gardens.

Lynes, Russell. *The Art-Makers of Nineteenth-Century America.* New York: Atheneum, 1970. Shows how American art-makers worked to change the climate of the arts in the nineteenth century, how they struggled to give their craft professional respectability.

Marx, Leo. *The Machine in the Garden: Technology and the Pastoral Ideal in America.* New York: Oxford University Press, 1964. Evaluates the uses of the pastoral ideal in the interpretation of our national experience, including its emergence as a distinctively American theory of society and its subsequent transformation under the impact of industrialism.

Matthiessen, F. O. *American Renaissance: Art and Expression in the Age of Emerson and Whitman.* New York: Oxford University Press, 1941. Deals with America's coming to its first maturity in the middle of the nineteenth century and affirming its rightful heritage in the whole expanse of art and culture.

Miller, Perry. *Nature's Nation.* Cambridge: Harvard University Press, 1967. A collection of essays dealing with the problem of American self-recognition, including the concerns of immigrants who, while clearly recognizing where they had come, still felt anxieties as to who they were.

Moore, Charles. *Daniel H. Burnham, Architect, Planner of Cities.* Boston: Houghton Mifflin, 1921. A detailed biography, giving ample coverage of Burnham's association with Olmsted during the planning of the World's Columbian Exposition.

Mumford, Lewis. *The Brown Decades: A Study of the Arts in America, 1865–1895.* New York: Harcourt Brace, 1931. Shows that the post–Civil War period contained the beginnings of a new integrity and power in American art, including the improvement of the landscape through the work of such men as George Perkins Marsh and Olmsted.

Nash, Roderick. *Wilderness and the American Mind.* New Haven: Yale University Press, 1967. The delineation and interpretation of the changing conception of wilderness as a basic ingredient of American civilization.

Newton, Norman T. *Design on the Land: The Development of Landscape Architecture.* Cambridge: Harvard University Press, 1971.

A comprehensive history of landscape architecture, and of its development as an art and as a profession, from ancient times to the present.

Novak, Barbara. *American Painting of the Nineteenth Century: Realism, Idealism, and the American Experience.* New York: Praeger, 1969. Establishes a perspective of ideas against which some of the more important American artists of the nineteenth century can be studied.

Pevsner, Nikolaus. *The Sources of Modern Architecture and Design.* London: Thames and Hudson, 1968. Describes certain nineteenth-century sources of twentieth-century architecture and design.

Ranney, Victoria Post. *Olmsted in Chicago.* Chicago: R. R. Donnelley, 1972. Olmsted's role as park designer for Chicago, as well as designer of the grounds for the World's Columbian Exposition.

Reed, Henry Hope, and Duckworth, Sophia. *Central Park: A History and a Guide.* 2d ed. New York: Clarkson N. Potter, 1972. A brief history (with illustrations) of Central Park, followed by proposed walking tours of both northern and southern sections plus miscellaneous information about the park.

Roper, Laura Wood. *FLO: A Biography of Frederick Law Olmsted.* Baltimore: Johns Hopkins University Press, 1973. A splendid, monumental biography of Olmsted's life and careers, indispensable to an understanding of its subject.

Russell, Carl P. *One Hundred Years in Yosemite: The Story of a Great Park and Its Friends.* Berkeley: University of California Press, 1947. An appraisal of the accomplishments of those, including Olmsted, who took the first steps in creating Yosemite and the National Parks movement.

Sax, Joseph L. "America's National Parks: Their Principles, Purposes, and Prospects." *National History Special Supplement,* October 1976, pp. 59–87. Traces the development of our national parks system from the creation of Yosemite as a state park during the Civil War, with special emphasis on Olmsted, John Muir, and Stephen Mather.

Schmitt, Peter J. *Back to Nature: The Arcadian Myth in Urban America.* New York: Oxford University Press, 1969. Argues that urbanization has not only refashioned the physical environment of townspeople but also profoundly altered the way they perceive the natural world outside the city.

Smith, Henry Nash. *Virgin Land: The American West as Symbol and Myth.* Cambridge: Harvard University Press, 1950. Traces the impact of the West on the consciousness of Americans, suggesting the principal consequences of this impact in literature and social thought.

Smithson, Robert. "Frederick Law Olmsted and the Dialectical Landscape." *Artforum* 11 (February 1973): 62–68. Argues that an Olmsted park should not be viewed as a "thing-in-itself" but rather as a process of ongoing relationships existing in a physical region.

Solotaroff, Theodore. "Alive and Together in the Park." *New York Times Magazine,* 13 June 1976. The diverse ways in which New Yorkers can enjoy themselves in Central Park and shake off the city's paranoia.

Stevenson, Elizabeth. *Park Maker: A Life of Frederick Law Olmsted.* New York: Macmillan, 1977. A full, vividly personalized biography of one of the lost heroes of American history, set against the background of the nineteenth century.

Strong, George Templeton. *The Diary of George Templeton Strong.* 4 vols. Edited by Allan Nevins and Milton Halsey Thomas. New York: Macmillan, 1952. A great diary, plainly written for posterity during the years 1835 to 1875, providing a sweeping panorama of social and political change in New York City.

Stroud, Dorothy. *Humphry Repton.* London: Country Life, 1962. The life and work of one of the outstanding figures in the English landscape garden movement, which flourished from 1720 to 1820.

Sullivan, Louis. *The Autobiography of an Idea.* New York: Press of the A.I.A., 1924. The story of Sullivan's life, setting forth his hopes, accomplishments, and philosophy and concluding with his appraisal of the World's Columbian Exposition.

Taylor, Lisa, ed. *Urban Open Spaces.* New York: Cooper-Hewitt Museum, the Smithsonian Institution's National Museum of Design, 1979. A collection of essays dealing with public outdoor spaces in large metropolitan centers, showing both the problems concerning their management and use and also the possibilities for improving them.

Tharp, Louise Hall. *Saint-Gaudens and the Gilded Era.* Boston: Little, Brown, 1969. The life of the famous sculptor set against the backdrop of the gilded era in New York City.

Tunnard, Christopher, and Reed, Henry Hope. *American Skyline: The Growth and Form of our Cities and Towns.* Boston: Houghton Mifflin, 1953. Describes how each new development in the history of the American city (from log cabins to skyscrapers) is the result of newly felt needs and desires of our people.

Tunnard, Christopher. *The City of Man.* 2d ed. New York: Charles Scribner's, 1970. A definition of the city in its economic, legal, and social aspects and a new theory of city planning based on the resources of architecture, landscape architecture, the decorative arts, and painting and sculpture.

Udall, Stewart L. *The Quiet Crisis.* New York: Holt, Rinehart and Winston, 1963. Describes the "quiet conservation crisis" of the 1960s, with a chapter, "Cities in Trouble," treating Olmsted as conservation prophet and master planner for urban America.

Vaux, Calvert. *Villas and Cottages.* New York: Harper, 1857. A series of designs for picturesque country houses by Olmsted's frequent collaborator.

Wurman, Richard S., Levy, Alan, and Katz, Joel. *The Nature of Recreation: A Handbook in Honor of Frederick Law Olmsted.* Cambridge, Mass.: MIT Press, 1972. A tribute to Olmsted, using his words and works as a starting point for an assessment of our recreational facilities and needs.

Index